The Zoni English System

Writing Team: Sultan Stover
Joel R. Nuñez
Evina B. Torres

Methodology Team: Sultan Stover
Evina B. Torres
Zoilo C. Nieto

Editor: Evina B. Torres
Zoilo C. Nieto

Directors: Zoilo C. Nieto
Evina B. Torres

ZONI™
ENGLISH
SYSTEM
A Unique Classroom Instructional Method™

Foreword

The Zoni English System has been designed as a classroom instructional method in response to the great need demonstrated by non-native speakers of English in their everyday lives in English-speaking countries.

Since communication is essential for survival, the Zoni English System method is based on daily life situations, while explaining fundamental expressions as well as grammatical structures. By doing so, we have also utilized high-frequency vocabulary. Effective textual materials increase the student's motivation to continue studying English by influencing his or her attitude toward learning as well as enhancing his or her future possibilities.

OBJECTIVES

Zoni English System 11 is designed to provide students with all the important skills in speech communication. Students are guided in learning the rudiments of speech writing and delivery specifically in informative, persuasive, and impromptu speeches, including debates. It helps them to present information, ideas and opinions in a coherent organized manner. There are sample models for each form of speech in each unit to be used as activities for critical thinking, vocabulary building and discussions. The exercises are geared to reinforce different skills such as writing, reading, listening and speaking.

A variety of creative and proven methodologies and strategies are implemented to enrich the teaching and learning experience, thereby achieving the Zoni English System objectives. One unique feature in this course is the use of audio/video recording as a tool in evaluating a student's progress in speech presentation.

TO THE TEACHER

<u>In the classroom</u>
Teacher talking time 10–30%
Student talking time 70–90%

Methodology and Techniques To Be Employed:
Instructors utilize such teaching techniques as:

- Ask & exchange
- Backward build-up drill
- Chain drill
- CIP (Choral Intonation Practice)
- Cloze exercise/fill in the blanks
- Concept-checking questions
- Contextualization
- Cooperative learning
- Conversation practice
- Debate
- Demonstration
- Dialogue practice
- Dictation
- Direct method
- Elicitation
- Elicitation through inference
- Error-correction
- Expansion/Drawing out activities
- Group work
- Horseshoe
- Hot seat
- Inferential questions
- Interactive reading
- Information gap
- Internet research
- Jigsaw
- Listen & repeat
- Multiple pair practice
- Multiple slot substitution
- Matching
- Open-ended story/Round Robin Storytelling
- Pair work
- Party time
- Peer correction
- Positive suggestion
- Project: individual/group
- Q & A (Question & Answer)
- Reading & listening
- Realia
- Role play
- Self-correction
- Sentence completion/transformation
- SPPD (Structure-Practice-Presentation-Dictation)
- Stand up activity
- Structure feedback
- Substitution drill

Teachers who have not gone through the Zoni co-teaching program are required to follow the methodology and techniques detailed in the **Zoni Teacher's Manual**.

Important Symbols:

Teachers consult the **Zoni Teacher's Manual** for instructions.

Teachers make groups of two students for **Pair Practice**.

Group Work is an activity for students in groups of three or more.

Audio/video recorder
Students must record all presentation activities from the book and all speeches which they are required to write and present. They must start from the self introduction which is more of a diagnostic procedure until the last speech to be delivered to monitor student's progress in oral presentation skills.

V | **Vocabulary** indicates the words and phrases which are used in all reading passages. Students must comprehend their meanings as well as use them in context by writing their own sentences and speeches.

W | **Writing** includes the technical aspects and the elements of writing presentations from introduction to conclusion for informative and persuasive speeches. Also, in the discussion of ideas in speeches for specific purposes such as debates.

S | **Speaking** helps students in delivering all types of presentations. It also engages them in conversation and discussion of all readings and activities.

L | **Listening** focuses more on comprehension of all speeches delivered by students, including presentation activities from the book.

Zoni English System 11 emphasizes writing and delivering speeches more, using Zoni's methodology and approaches such as: cooperative learning, pair & group work discussion, internet research and using audio and visual aids. This increased importance placed on student-centered learning in the Zoni classroom supports the enhanced and simultaneous usage of all four language skills. Each student is given greater amounts of class time to practice the target language, thereby maximizing student learning and progress in the classroom.

CLASSROOM SEATING ARRANGEMENTS

In addition to applying various teaching methodologies, teachers are also encouraged to vary their classroom seating arrangements based on the lesson. The number of students and class size are factors that will also help to determine the seating arrangements.

Standard

This type of seating arrangement, where students are arranged in rows, is generally used for lecture-type lessons and presentations. It is also beneficial when we need all the students to be focused on a particular task on the board. Students are able to work at their own pace while doing their assignments. It tends to be teacher-centered. The teacher must circulate and make lots of eye contact with his/her students to ensure all are involved in the assigned task.

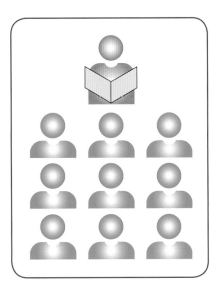

In the Zoni System, lessons generally begin with the standard seating arrangement, especially during the introduction of a grammar point.

Semi-Circle

This seating arrangement is recommended when maximum student interaction is required to focus on a particular task, such as getting information from the board or audio-visual activities and exercises. Students are able to see their classmates' gestures and facial expressions easily during discussions. In addition, it is less teacher-centered, so it provides lots of student interaction.

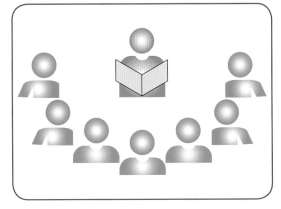

Circle: Group Work

Group work generally consists of three or more students, and is designed for maximum student participation. Students are more relaxed about experimenting with the language and the fear of making mistakes is diminished. Group work is a cooperative learning experience where students learn from one another. Group work becomes very effective when the groups are given clear instructions, tasks related to the objective of the lesson, and a specific allotment of time in which to complete the assigned tasks.

Pair Work

Pair Work has the same conditions as group work but with two students.

In the lower and intermediate levels, the Zoni System incorporates a lot of group work and/or pair work during the practice period sessions.

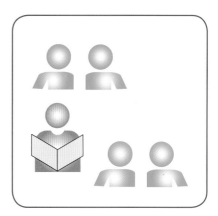

Homework

When we assign homework to students, it is important that we also check it in the following class. Checking homework should not take more than 15 minutes. Make sure you check all students' homework, but vary your homework-checking routine; for example, check it in the second hour of class. Finally, keep a record of which students have not done their homework. For each assignment not completed, a student gets a zero. Alert any student who receives a lot of homework zeroes, as he or she may have to repeat the course.

SURPRISE FACTOR

Though developing a routine in the classroom is good, at other times, it is critical that teachers change their classroom routines to keep students on their toes.
Some ways to use the surprise factor are:

1. Checking the homework in the second hour of the class period instead of at the beginning of the class period.

2. Asking the class a question, then zeroing in and calling on a student to answer it.

INDISPENSABLE ORAL PRACTICE

The Zoni English System encourages choral and individual repetition in order to improve the students' pronunciation and to help them lose any fear of the language. Teachers should not be reluctant to practice pronunciation even with upper-level students; all students at any level benefit from this frequent practice. Teachers should also ensure that students keep their books closed and do not take notes during the introduction of a new subject or during oral practice. Their focus must remain on the task and subject matter.

ELICITATION FROM THE STUDENTS

Take advantage of students' prior knowledge by eliciting vocabulary and examples from them. By doing so, students share their knowledge with the rest of the class, build confidence, promote active thinking, and stimulate students to come up with interesting examples.

BOARD WORK

At Zoni, we believe in keeping board work as simple as possible, especially when teaching the beginner and intermediate levels. Board work is beneficial in that teachers can use it as a resource for student practice when doing Choral Intonation Practice (CIP), drilling and role playing. Board work keeps students focused, and reinforces reading and spelling.

While doing board work, make sure all students have their books and notebooks closed. No writing or copying is allowed during this period. All students must be focused on the board. Write in print, not cursive. Plan what you will be putting on the board ahead of time. If writing a long dialogue, work your dialogue one segment at a time. We strongly recommend that teachers follow our board work examples displayed in the **Zoni Teacher's Manual**.

ATTENDANCE

Learning English is a matter of constant and consistent practice and dedication. Student attendance is vital for maximum learning and benefit; this is why teachers must remind students that regular attendance is necessary. If students do not comply, they may be asked to take the course again. Attendance should not be taken for granted. Encouragement and reminders about class attendance are essential.

ACKNOWLEDGMENTS

We are very pleased and proud to announce the publication of a new book in the Zoni English System series: *Zoni English System 11*. The experience of constantly challenging the status quo has led to the creation of this book. Many people have been involved in this project; their passion, persistence, dedication, and teamwork made it possible to complete *Zoni English System 11*. We would like to thank **Miyuki Adachi** for her exceptional graphic design work that consistently enhances the Zoni teaching and learning experience. We would also like to thank **Eric Jonas** and **Max E Sanchez** for their valuable input. We very much appreciate the cooperation and suggestions of the Zoni faculty. In addition, we would like to recognize the contributions of Zoni students who have provided us with much-needed feedback.

Zoilo C. Nieto & Evina B. Torres
Directors

Table of Contents

Unit 2 | PUBLIC SPEAKING

59

Unit 3 | PERSUASIVE SPEECH

93

Unit 4 | SPEAKING FOR SPECIFIC PURPOSES

139

Unit 5 | WRITE, EDIT and PRESENT

177

Appendix | Effective Speech Delivery Forms

The forms are to be used consistently in evaluating the speeches and presentations of students. By doing this, the students will be guided through the principles of speech communication, thereby making them more aware of their strengths as well as areas for improvement, as they deliver their actual presentations. The teacher will be more aware of the progress of the student's ability in oral presentation skills.

Dear Zoni Student

We would like to welcome you to *Zoni English System 11*. In order to get the most out of your study of English, you should always do the following:

- Speak only English in class.
- Attend class every day.
- Do all assigned homework.
- Do all presentation activities.
- Record all presentations for speech evaluation purposes.
- *Relax and have fun!*

Unit 1

INTRODUCTION

" You can speak well if your tongue can deliver the message of your heart."

John Ford

 WARM UP ACTIVITY

A Look at the picture on page 2 and explain your responses for the following questions.

1. What do you think he might be speaking about?

2. Is he talking about a person, place, thing, or memorable event in his life, or about himself?

3. What do you want people to know about you?

4. Do you like to tell people about yourself? On what occasions?

PRESENTATION ACTIVITY

See Teacher's Manual

Let's start with a very easy topic to develop: introducing yourself. What could be easier to talk about than yourself, right? However, because you are very familiar with yourself, you might end up talking about yourself in a very *haphazard* fashion. A good way to approach this first activity, therefore, is to focus on one aspect of your life that you would like to talk about that would be interesting for you and your audience. Remember, if your topic is not interesting to you, it won't be interesting to your audience, either.

Let us examine this speech prepared by a former Zoni student, Arackaparambil Kurian Pillai Balaram.

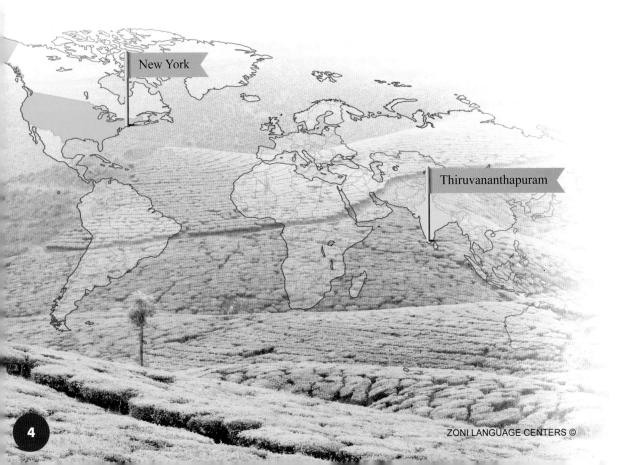

New York

Thiruvananthapuram

Tiruvananthapuram *(handwritten)*

SPEECH DIAGNOSTIC
Example "Self-Introduction"

Why Am I Here? Why I Am Here

My name is Arackaparambil Kurian Pillai Balaram, and I am from Thiruvananthapuram, India. Quite a *mouthful* for a first introduction. You can call me Bill, which is my chosen Western name for my Western friends. You can call my city by its English equivalent, Trivandrum. My hometown is located in the southwestern part of India, and is the capital city of the State of Kerala. I have brought with me a map so you can see where Trivandrum is.

As you can see, it is quite far in relation to New York. To get here, our family travelled a total of 35 hours. It could have taken only 20 hours, but my father is a proud Indian. He wanted to travel only on Air India, and from Trivandrum we had to stop over in Kochi, then in Delhi, before finally arriving in New York. It was an exhausting trip, and although we arrived two weeks ago, I believe my jet lag is still around, so please forgive me if I seem boring today. Quite honestly, I am quite jolly on most days.

I am here now in New York City because my father is a doctor undergoing further education in his field of **ophthalmology**. You see, India has a large population of people who are unable to get medical services because of many factors: poverty, limited access to medical facilities, and sadly, ignorance. My father did not want anyone in my family—my mother, myself and my little sister—to be left behind in India while he undergoes his training for the next 18 months. My mother is a teacher in India and my sister and I are being home-schooled based on our own educational system.

The English that I know is quite different from the English that I am learning now. India was a colony of Great Britain and as such, we have been taught British English. I find English **stodgy**, which is why I enjoy learning American English, which is more fluid, relaxed and casual.

It is only the first week of school and already I have made friends with my teachers and most of you, my classmates. I am happy with this class, because there are only a few of us in the class, giving us more time to interact with our teacher.

However, I need to **bone up on** my English, which is why I am now taking this wonderful ESL class at Zoni.

I miss home, my friends, and our garden where my sister and I could play, and where my school friends come over for a snack of gulab jamun. Oddly, however, I am happy to be here. I have my new friends to keep me entertained and help me with my English.

CLASS ACTIVITY   V S L

B Group Work: **In groups of three, go over Bill's speech again and share your opinion about it.**

1. Is it a good speech?

2. What is good about it? What did you not like about his speech?

3. If Bill were with you now, and he asked for your help, how would you help him improve his speech?

See Teacher's Manual

PRESENTATION ACTIVITY   S L

C Write something about yourself. Imagine that you were invited by your friend to attend a casual or formal party. What would you like the other guest to know about you? Deliver a two minute self introduction. Try to memorize it.

My name is Luis but I like to be called Tony because is second name. I'm from Guatemala I came to N.Y. many years ago was not easy to come here, now I'm here, the first year was tough when I came here, because I missed a lot of my family, friends, but I'm happy, because I have new friends. They are like my family

READING EXERCISE

Phobias

The human mind is a world rich with many possibilities. In it thrives unlimited imagination and potential, power and strength. On the other hand, the human mind could also be an insecure host of a number of fears or phobias. Some of them are reasonable and considered common phobias such as claustrophobia, achluophobia and altophobia. There are also some unreasonable or weird fears such as acerophobia or the fear of sourness, nelophobia or the fear of glass, and thaasophobia, which is the fear of sitting. Can you even believe these phobias exist? Do you think fear is part of human nature?

One example of a reasonable phobia which most of us have experienced is aviatophobia better known as the fear of flying. At one time or another, we may have taken a turbulent flight, causing us to believe that the plane was close to crashing. Reading about plane crashes or seeing movies about them doesn't help us to overcome this fear. The famous American Queen of Soul, Aretha Franklin, never flies. She travels around the United States in a custom-made bus that has all the comforts that someone of her *stature* is used to. Instead of overcoming her aviatophobia—her fear of flying—she has instead done something to avoid flying *altogether*.

Aretha Franklin

Pair Practice

D **Pair Work:** **Read the passage and study the different types of fears or phobias identified in it. Discuss the following questions with your partner.**

1. Do you have any fears?
2. What are they? Can you name five of them?
3. Rank them from one to five, one being the worst.

List of Phobias:
1. Achluophobia—Fear of darkness
2. Arophobia/Altrophobia—Fear of heights
3. Claustrophobia—Fear of confined spaces
4. Homophobia—Fear of becoming homosexual
5. Hydrophobia—Fear of water
6. Hemaphobia/hemophobia/Hematophobis—fear of blood
7. Gerascophobia—Fear of growing old
8. Photophobia—Fear of lights
9. Philophobia—Fear of falling in love or being in love
10. Plutophobia—Fear of wealth
11. Sociophobia—Fear of society or people in general
12. Verbophobia—Fear of word
13. Xenoglossophobia—Fear of foreign language
14. Xenophobia—Fear of strangers or foreigners

 **PARTY TIME** [S]

E Group Work/Party Time: **Interview your classmates about their fears using the following interview guide questions**

1. What are your five worst fears?
2. When did you start to experience them?
3. Have you overcome your fears? How have you *coped* with them?
4. Did someone help you deal with your fears? Who was it?
5. What advice can you give someone who has a really terrible fear?
6. What are the most common fears in the United States?

TRIVIA

The survey enumerates the top 10 human fears.
Guess what the number one fear is?

Mario	Emma	María	Wang
Death	insects	height	Ghost
300	800	500	400

Not death, which ranks sixth, or insects, which come in third. According to David Wallechinsky, The Book of Lists, the No. 1 fear is the fear of speaking in public. Can you believe this?

Stage fright is the worst fear according to a survey conducted among Americans. So, if you wrote down public speaking as your No. 1 fear, you're in good company. Welcome to the world of glossophobia. Thankfully, even if stage fright or the fear of speaking in public is on top of the list for 75% of people surveyed for phobias, it is one that can be overcome. As with other phobias, the key to overcoming stage fright is understanding what it is and what causes it. Getting over phobias could be easily done with proper managing and understanding.

HOW DO I KNOW IF I HAVE STAGE FRIGHT?

SELF-EVALUATION:

Q. When you introduced yourself did you have stage fright? Ask yourself the following questions and try to answer them as honestly as you can.

1. Do you experience extreme anxiety or fear before you go onstage to deliver a speech? Does the mere thought of speaking in public fill you with fear, even if it's just in a small classroom with a few students?

2. Do you physically get ill when you are about to speak in public?

3. Do you break out in a sweat at the thought of facing an audience?

4. Do you *have butterflies in your stomach* prior to a speaking activity?

If you experience any or ALL of these symptoms, then you have stage fright.

WHY DO PEOPLE HAVE STAGE FRIGHT?

There are many reasons why people experience stage fright. Some may have developed this out of a traumatic childhood experience related to speaking in public. For example, if a young child is laughed at or made fun of while, or after, performing in public.

Others may have a low sense of self-confidence when it comes to public speaking, and this *triggers* the fear. It is worth pointing out that people with a high sense of self-confidence in other matters would actually *buckle under* the pressure of speaking in public.

READING EXERCISE   V   S   L

F Pair Work: **Read the following story in pairs, then answer the comprehension questions. Take note of the bold-faced words and try to define them yourselves by using contextual clues.**

STAGE ACTOR'S NIGHTLY ROUTINE

When I was a *scrawny* and *bespectacled* young man, I was part of a professional theater company that regularly produced shows for a paying audience. It was a fun activity and it earned me some *pocket change* while I was in college. Moreover, I got to meet really interesting, and sometimes, famous people in the cast.

Once, the company decided to put on the musical ANNIE. I *auditioned* for a role and got a part in the chorus. The actor who played Daddy Warbucks, the billionaire who adopts Annie, was a famous movie and TV actor and we were excited to work with him. Because of his fame, we were all in awe of him. Despite his fame, he was very professional and worked very hard at each rehearsal. He was also a *jovial* guy who did not act like he was a big star, and was friendly with us unknowns. After only a few days of rehearsals, he had the part *down pat*. He was truly an inspiration to all of us.

After weeks of rehearsals, it was finally time to hold our technical and dress rehearsal with an audience. We were all thrilled to be performing before an audience. Following our routine, we warmed up by doing some stretching exercises, and ran through our vocalization routine to prepare for all the singing that we were about to do. After the warm-ups, we each went to our own corner to have a little quiet time before the show. I was observing a lot of the people in our cast and everyone looked *primed* to do our opening number. As I looked around, I noticed that our big star, the movie and TV actor, was nowhere to be found. I nearly panicked! The show was about to start! I *made a beeline for* our changing room to look for our star. Where could he be? The changing room was empty.

Then, all of a sudden, I heard a *muffled* sound coming from the shower room. It sounded like someone behind the door was *retching* in dry

heaves. I knocked softly on the door, and asked, "Is everything all right?" I heard *mumbling* from within, and after a few nervous seconds, the door opened and out came our star, with a *sheepish* look on his face. He said, "I'm OK. It's just that opening night always *gives me the jitters*." He continued to tell me that ever since he was a young man, he always had the worst case of stage fright before each performance, especially on opening night, and that it gets so bad that he throws up before going onstage. He *assured* me however, that everything was all right. We went backstage together, just in time for the opening number. A star? With stage fright? It was unbelievable!

Onstage, our star gave a *flawless* performance. He did not *manifest* an *iota* of nervousness all throughout, from his first entrance, all the way to the final number.

When we took our bows to the *raucous* applause of the audience, our star gave me a thumbs-up sign. Everything was going great for now, but I know that in the next performances, our star would *succumb* to his nightly routine before going onstage.

COMPREHENSION QUESTIONS

G Answer the following comprehension questions.

1. Did the author act for a living? What part of the story gives you the answer?

2. Why do you think the author was very impressed with the movie and TV actor?

3. What was the routine that all the actors in the theater company did before each performance? Contrast this with the star's "routine."

4. Do you have a personal way of coping with stage fright?

VOCABULARY IN CONTEXT

H Pair Work: **In pairs, read the following sentences and use contextual clues to define the bold-faced words.**

1. Jessica was so mad at the motorist who drove in a *haphazard* way ahead of her, because he/she zigzagged between lanes thoughtlessly.

_____

_____

2. When Mio was still a new actor, he found each line in the script to be a *mouthful* and difficult to say and memorize.

_____

_____

_____

3. Terry specialized in **ophthalmology** because she wants to follow in the footsteps of her country's National Hero, Dr. Jose P. Rizal.

_____

_____

_____

_____

4. Tim couldn't sit still in church because he thought that the sermon was **stodgy** and uninteresting.

_____

_____

5. Isha helped her brother **bone up on** his dancing because he had trouble learning the steps at first, and was going to a dance on Friday.

_____

_____

_____

_____

6. It is not unusual for someone **to get butterflies** in his stomach even for the simplest speaking chores, such as talking to the teacher to discuss something simple.

_____

_____

7. As a young boy, Kohsuke ate too little and played too much, which is why he was very **scrawny.**

_____

_____

8. Shinsuke likes wearing eyeglasses because people immediately think that **bespectacled** people are smart.

_____

_____

_____

9. Marta told Fernando that if the money someone owes him is just **pocket change**, he shouldn't bother collecting it, even if it remains unpaid.

_____

_____

_____

10. Many famous actors like Paul Newman **auditioned** many times for minor roles before they landed their first major acting assignment.

_____

_____

11. Min really admires people who remain *jovial*, no matter the stressful conditions that surround them.

_____

_____

12. It was only after hours and hours of studying that Stephen had all of the idioms in the book *down pat*. Now, it is very easy and natural for him to use these expressions.

_____

_____

13. Omar got a high score on his Architecture History class because he *primed* himself by visiting famous landmarks in New York.

_____

_____

14. When Napassorn saw Psy in Times Square, she *made a beeline for* him, so she could get his autograph.

_____

_____

15. Although the sounds coming from his neighbor's apartment were *muffled*, Mateo still couldn't concentrate on his homework so he went and asked her to please be quiet.

_____

_____

16. The sight of dead bodies makes me *retch.*

_____

_____

17. "I would be *sheepish* too if I needed a big favor from my boss," said Juanra to his co-worker.

_____

_____

18. Before he got married to Jessica, Marcelo admitted that he had a bit of the *jitters*.

_____

_____

_____

_____

19. Although nothing was put down in writing, Graciela's landlord *assured* her that he would not be raising the rent this year.

_____

_____

_____

_____

20. Elena's rendition of the American jazz classic Summertime was *flawless*, which is why she was highly praised for her singing.

_____

_____

21. Even if Sebastien was very nervous to meet his future in-laws, he did not *manifest* any signs of this because he wanted the dinner with them and his fiancée to be perfect.

_____

_____

22. The lawsuit against the suspect was immediately dismissed because there was not an *iota* of evidence to convict him.

_____

_____

23. New Year's Eve, St. Patrick's Day and Halloween are among the most *raucous* festivities held in New York.

_____

_____

24. Although she is on a diet, Suk Lee will *succumb* to the temptation of eating an extra éclair because it is her favorite pastry.

_____

_____

_____

HOW CAN WE OVERCOME STAGE FRIGHT?

Pair Practice

See Teacher's Manual

1 Pair Work: **Discuss the following phrases with your partner and choose the five most appropriate things to do when speaking in public.**

1. smile at your audience

2. take a deep breath and breathe naturally

3. say hum…. hum……

4. make yourself comfortable for three-five minutes before delivering your speeches

5. wipe your face and hands because you are sweating

6. crack a joke before delivering your main speech

7. identify the person whom you would like to have eye contact with

8. say sorry when you stammer

9. practice before delivering your speech

10. apologize first if there are points that you have forgotten

To deal with stage fright, you must get to its **root cause** or causes. If a childhood **trauma** prevents you from speaking in public, you must examine why you were laughed at or made fun of: was it because you were not prepared? If so, try to spend more time preparing for a speaking engagement. Having someone listen to you and give you constructive criticism is a good way to **gauge** whether you are ready to face your audience.

If your issue is lack of self-confidence, ask yourself why. More often than not, our **insecurities** have no real basis. After you identify the cause of your insecurity, ask someone to listen to your presentation so you will **have a sense** of whether you are doing well or not.

In either case, your best friend in overcoming your glossophobia is practice, practice, and more practice!

There are many ways to deal with stage fright, and I would like to share some of the best tips that I have come across:

Off the top of your head, who do you think are the people who need to deal with stage fright on almost a daily basis? Would you say it's your doctor? Your parents? Your co-workers? What if I were to suggest one answer: PERFORMERS. Their profession is one that requires them to be in front of an audience. If they are stage actors or concert musicians, they do this as part of their **daily grind**. For movie or TV actors, they have to **subject themselves to** the **scrutiny** of the TV or movie crew during the shoot, and the further inspection of their movie or TV audience, **not to mention** critics. Such a life must be **unnerving**, **to say the least**.

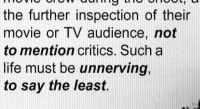

ACKNOWLEDGE:
Find a *common denominator*

Read through the interviews about *coping* with stage fright. There seems to be a common denominator among all of them, can you find it?

1. Do not focus on yourself. Focus on your presentation.

The **trick** to doing away with stage fright is to shift the focus away from you, the person, the very same one who has to deal with stage fright. You are not presenting yourself, but are creating a performance for your audience. If you focus on yourself, you will just have butterflies in your stomach.

Jason Alexander

*Seinfeld stars**

The actor Jason Alexander, who appeared in the hit TV series *SEINFELD* and in the American classic *PRETTY WOMAN*, recounts how he was able to deal with his stage fright:

"I had a wonderful acting teacher who I **confided** in about this experience. He told me that he believed that kind of **debilitating** fear was a result of misplaced ego. He used to say, "Jason, these people are not here to see you; they don't really care about you. They are here to see the story. Just tell them the story.""

"Just tell them the story. Big idea. When I began to make the story the most important thing, I became much less the focus of my concerns. I realized that I was one small element on the stage, working with my colleagues to tell our audience a story. The information is what people want, the experience is what they want. They're not there for me. They would be just as happy having someone else tell them the story. The material—the work—is everything."

* *Jason Alexander (left), Jerry Seinfeld, Julia Louis-Dreyfus & Michael Richards*

2. Anticipate some mistakes to happen.

It is a sad reality that nothing and no one is perfect. While it is good to think positively, it is also reasonable to keep a level head when it comes to your presentation. There will be good days, and some days will be *off*. Prepare for when things *go south*, and when they do, do not make the further mistake of *telegraphing* your *blunder* to your audience. Unless you really mess up, chances are, your audience will not know you made a mistake, unless you show them that you have. Even the best public speakers commit the occasional *gaffe* at some point. The difference between a good speaker and a bad one is how one handles a mistake.

3. Just think that your audience wants you to succeed

Put yourself in the shoes of your audience. Do you think you're a better speaker than the person onstage? More likely than not, you are not. The person onstage is scared, just as you would be if you were onstage. Both you and the speaker know what it is like to be onstage. Your heart goes to the speaker. You wish him nothing but success. You admire him for having the *guts* to speak in public. You therefore take his side. You want him to succeed. Now switch places. Now that you are about to speak, think that your audience wants you to succeed. They will forgive any slight slipup you might commit. They will be *lenient*. They are on your side.

4. There is such a thing as over-preparation.

Over-compensation is a common problem, especially for beginners. Their reason for doing this is usually to make sure that their presentation is perfect. Do you remember what we read a few paragraphs back? It is a sad reality that nothing and no one is perfect. A speaker who over-prepares is just showing his insecurity. Since there is no such thing as perfect, then the speaker who over-prepares is bound to fail.

Over-preparation also leads to over-speaking. Your presentation should contain only the most important points that will allow your audience to appreciate what you're trying to say to them. If you say enough, then your audience will think that you did a good job. If you say too much, your audience will just end up being bored. A ***seasoned*** speaker knows where to draw the line between being prepared and being too prepared.

5. Get help

Put yourself in the shoes of your audience. Having someone to help us get through our public speaking fears is a good way to approach this problem. There are professional counselors who will help you get your act together, but if one is too expensive or is otherwise not available, then you can approach your teacher, or a co-worker, a classmate or a family member to listen to your presentation as some sort of a test audience. It is possible that by overcoming your fear of public speaking with just a test audience could be the first step to overcoming your fear of public speaking altogether.

❓ COMPREHENSION QUESTIONS

J Pair Work: **In pairs answer the following questions.**

1. Do you agree or disagree with the following statements?
You can never prepare too much for a speech or a presentation.
The key to becoming an effective public speaker is to prepare,
prepare and prepare again. Explain your arguments.

2. Do most experienced speakers agree that it is all right to be nervous
before they speak?

3. Is it true that you should fear making a mistake?

🔤 VOCABULARY IN CONTEXT

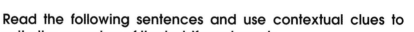

K Read the following sentences and use contextual clues to
write the meaning of the boldfaced words.

1. Julie's *daily grind* consists of a home-to-work-to-home routine.

_____

_____

2. To make sure that all their products are the best, Apple puts each
one through the strictest *scrutiny* before sending them to their stores.

_____

_____

3. Drinking too much alcohol causes a lot of health problems, *not to
mention* social problems.

_____

_____

4. It was *unnerving* for Hiroko to meet her high school classmate here in New York.

_____

_____

_____

5. Tetsu's decision to get married at 21 years old shocked his classmates, *to say the least*.

_____

_____

6. Evelyn was still *coping* with the death of her puppy, which is why we did not talk about our own pets, so as not to upset her.

_____

_____

7. The *common denominator* that defines this class is our common desire to learn English as a second language.

_____

_____

8. The *trick* to making the best brownies is to use only imported chocolate powder.

_____

_____

9. José **confided** in Carolina that he was the one who hid Carlos' phone as a prank.

_____

_____

10. Many people believe that if another tax crisis comes up, it would have **debilitating** effects on their personal finances.

_____

_____

11. Something is **off** with this sandwich: it has a very peculiar smell and taste.

_____

_____

12. Choi is an entrepreneur and he will never allow his business to **go south**.

_____

_____

13. Yvonne giggled after the actor forgot his lines because he **telegraphed** his mistake. It was so obvious.

_____

_____

14. Everyone agrees that Elsa committed a **blunder** when she broke off her engagement to such a great guy.

_____

_____

15. Being a new employee, it was understandable for Andres to commit a *gaffe* here and there on his first day on the job.

_____

_____

16. It took a lot of *guts* for Anabel to go bungee jumping from a 150-foot high bridge.

_____

_____

17. Thank God Makiko's parents are *lenient*. Otherwise, she would have been punished for using her dad's car without his prior permission.

_____

_____

18. Franklin's doctor said that it is *over-compensation* if a wealthy person tries to be simple when he is with ordinary people.

_____

_____

19. Tess is such a *seasoned* cook. She prepared dinner for eight people seemingly with no effort at all.

_____

_____

_____

THE TOOLS OF PUBLIC SPEAKING:
Non-verbal aspects of public speaking

Public speaking needs more than just the speaker, or just the speech. Public speaking **encompasses** many elements, each dependent on the others, with each being as important as the rest. Master these tools and you will become a master public speaker.

"Public speaking is listening to a speaker talk about his/her chosen topic. If he/she has a good voice that can be heard by everyone, then he/she is a good speaker." Do you agree with this statement?

If you answered, no, then you are...RIGHT! Confused? Well, don't be. What this means is simply this: Public speaking is not just about a speech, but it encompasses the speech, how the speaker says it, and how his/her audience sees him/her when he/she is presenting it. Speech, therefore, is both verbal and non-verbal communication.

We have already discussed the verbal part of public speaking. We have discussed how to plan and write a speech. Now let's deal with the non-verbal aspect of public speaking.

 WARM UP ACTIVITY   S   L

 Group Work: **In groups of three, discuss the following questions.**

1. Describe the people in the picture.
2. What do you think they are doing? Are they acting or delivering a speech?
3. What do you think is the best picture when speaking in public? Why?
4. How do you establish eye contact?
5. What is your idea of a good posture in public speaking?
6. Do audio visuals create a strong impact when delivering speeches? Why? Why not?
7. What is the tone and level of speech that is considered as a powerful voice? Who among the American Presidents has the most powerful voice? Is it Obama, Reagan, Clinton or G. W. Bush? Who is the best orator? Explain your choices.

1. BODY LANGUAGE AND GESTURES

A speaker's body language and gestures enrich an oral presentation, and allow him/her to punctuate important parts with hand and body movements that match the message. Using gestures also gives the speaker an aura of self-confidence, of being prepared and comfortable with himself/herself, his/her presentation and his audience.

Using too little is just as a bad as using too much body language. Gestures which a speaker should avoid are:

- Gestures that seem to show aggression, such as chopping motions and pointing towards the audience.
- An open palm should be used rather than a pointing finger to emphasize a point or when gesturing towards the audience.
- Crossing one's arms in front of one.
- Scratching one's head or any other part of one's body.
- Covering one's mouth and keeping one's hands clasped behind one's back.
- Speaking with one's back to the audience, unless necessary, and if so, one is not to stay in this position for too long.

2. EYE CONTACT

To a good number of seasoned public speakers, eye contact is the most basic element in public speaking, for many reasons. For one, a speaker who is comfortable with eye contact is comfortable with himself/herself, and by extension, his/her audience. A speaker who has no *qualms* making eye contact is a speaker who has self-confidence.

Secondly, establishing eye contact establishes trust. This is true not only with public speaking but with all human interaction. "Look at me in the eye" is a common command that is spoken by one person to test another person's sincerity. If you can do this without any discomfort, then you are a person who is telling the truth, and can therefore be trusted.

Bear in mind that effective eye contact does not mean that you have to stare at your audience the entire time that you are speaking. An effective speaker makes effective eye contact by looking at his/her audience every once in a while, instead of looking out into space or looking at his/her speech the entire time.

Rules to remember:

• Every member of your audience is important. Whether your audience is a small or big group, do not overlook any part of it. Establish and maintain eye contact with your audience in general, not just one or a few.

• Eye contact should be comfortable for both the speaker and his/her audience.

• Hold eye contact for as long as your audience maintains eye contact with you. Sometimes though, you should not hold eye contact for far too long. Through time, you will learn when eye contact needs to be broken. Be *mindful* that sometimes, holding eye contact for far too long becomes uncomfortable, and in some instances, *inappropriate*. The *rule of thumb* is this: if you feel comfortable holding a stare, you're on the right track, and *vice versa*.

• If you need to read from your notes when you are delivering a speech, make sure that you take time for both reading your notes AND maintaining eye contact. Reading too much from notes could be taken to mean insecurity on the part of the speaker.

3. POSTURE

One of America's greatest presidents was Abraham Lincoln. He was a **behemoth** in every sense of the word: standing at 6' 4" (1.93 m). He and Lyndon B. Johnson were the tallest American Presidents. But beyond his physical stature, Lincoln made his mark on American history with his many accomplishments, **chief** among which was to abolish slavery and finally reunite the Confederate States into the United States of America. He was also known as an accomplished orator, and his Gettysburg Address is considered a masterpiece. Although he did not have an impressive voice, Lincoln made up for this with his formidable height, which he used to maximum effect by standing erect at all times. His posture, confident and assured, captivated audiences and commanded their attention. By maintaining his posture at all times, his audience saw in Lincoln the leadership that was needed at one of America's darkest times.

4. | VISUAL AIDS

In the past, coming up with visual aids to enhance a presentation was a time-consuming activity. One had to ***grab*** as many newspapers and magazines as one could, ***pore over*** those publications page by page, hoping that he could find pictures and illustrations that could be used for one's presentation. If this was not enough, the speaker would have to make one's own visual aids: cutouts, drawings, etc.

Now, however, all a researcher needs to do is to turn on his/her computer and do an image search, and voila. Endless materials for a PowerPoint-assisted presentation pop up. If PowerPoint is too boring for you, you could also explore prezi.com, whose application makes for a zippier visual complement to your oral presentation. While there is nothing wrong with using images grabbed from the Internet, please do not forget to acknowledge or cite the author of the downloaded material.

Rules to remember when using visual aids:

• Make sure to edit visual presentations so that they will be in sync with your speech. Neither should be longer than the other.
• Visual aids should be well-organized so that what you are saying will match what your audience will be seeing and hearing.
• Do not read the text that is written on the visual aids. There is nothing more boring than watching a speaker reading off the screen or his notes, and what he/she is saying is exactly what is shown on screen. Remember, visual aids complement and supplement your speech. It is NOT the speech.

A speech with complete and interesting information captivates the speaker's audience, but one complemented with eye-catching visual aids will even reel in your audience even more. Visual aids become all the more important in speeches that are highly descriptive. Visual aids should, however, be utilized with the main speech in mind. They cannot be random or irrelevant and visual aids should be used only in parts of the speech that would do well with an illustration.

For example, in the speech about President Obama's popularity with young people, a pie chart illustrating the composition of the age groups that voted for him would help drive home the point that indeed, the younger vote constituted a huge chunk of the votes that went to him.

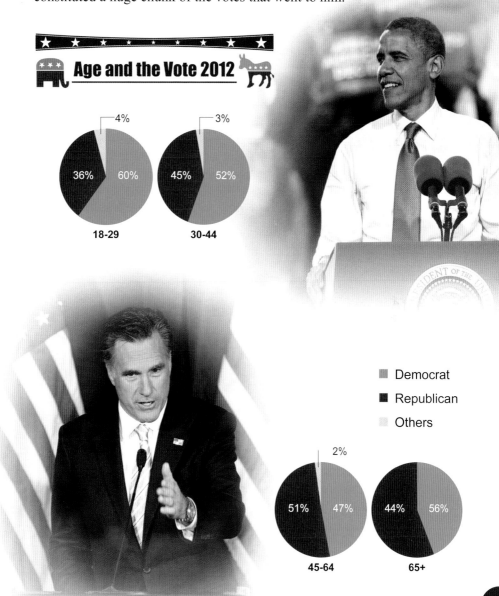

If you are talking about an interesting attraction of your country and you feel not too many in your class know where your country is, then use a map so people would be able to compare the relative distance of your country to theirs and the United States, as well as to identify its very location. Additionally, you may want to show a picture or several stunning photographs of the place that will be described in your speech.

You may even bring the very items that are the subject of your speech. I had a class where a student from Japan spoke about kimonos and mentioned that a good kimono could cost a lot. There was a stunned reaction from some people in the class because the amount seemed unbelievable. The speaker then took out her own kimono, and explained that it was made by hand and was customized, hence the exorbitant cost. The students saw up close how intricate and rich the embroidery and fabric were.

With the popularity of tablets, speakers are no longer tied down in their ability to present visual aids. Images could be searched and downloaded easily, then shared with the audience.

5. | FACIAL EXPRESSION and VOICE

William Shakespeare, the greatest English playwright who has ever lived, wrote this line in A MIDSUMMER NIGHT'S DREAM, "The eye of man hath not heard, the ear of man hath not seen…" Some *interpret* this to mean that when we speak we must appeal also to the eyes, and when we are seen, we must also appeal to the ears. In other words, a speaker must seem animated when delivering his/her presentation. A speaker needs to look interesting and interested. A good way to find out if you are doing things the right way is for you to practice in front of a mirror to gauge how effective your use of facial expressions is. Once you are comfortable with yourself, you may want to have someone check your facial expressions out.

Not everyone possesses a powerful voice. But everyone can speak with a clear voice. If made to choose between a speaker with a big voice but unclear speech, and another who speaks clearly with a moderate voice, who would you rather listen to?

Speech experts say that when one delivers a speech, he/she should speak as if he/she is speaking to the person in the last row. This way, the speaker ensures that everyone in his/her audience, from the first to the last row, will hear him/her clearly.

VOCABULARY IN CONTEXT   V W

Read the following sentences and use contextual clues to write the meaning of the boldfaced words.

1. Shota was surprised that Kevin had no *qualms* about eating narezushi, even if its main ingredient is fermented fish. On the other hand, I hesitated.

_____

_____

2. Anastacia is very forgetful, so she has to *bear in mind* that she may end up neglecting to do what she's supposed to do. Perhaps she should write notes to help her remember those tasks.

_____

_____

3. The first time she came to New York, Boots was always careful to be always *mindful* of what was happening around her. Because she was always aware of her surroundings, she never had any unpleasant experiences.

_____

_____

4. Antonio showed up for the barbecue in a tuxedo. He knew the attire was *inappropriate* but he wanted to play a prank on his friends.

_____

_____

5. A good *rule of thumb* when converting meters to feet is to divide a meter by 3. It might not be 100% correct, but it's a good way to make an estimate.

_____

_____

6. When baking a cake using a mix, it does not matter if you put the mix before the eggs or *vice versa*. The result will still be good either way.

_____

_____

7. Once she saw the roller coaster at Six Flags, Valeria cried out, "Oh my God! There is no way I am going to ride that *behemoth*! It is just too big and scary!"

_____

_____

8. The *chief* reason why Victor moved to New York was to pursue further studies in architecture. There were other reasons, but they were secondary.

_____

_____

9. Kris *grabbed* lots of freebies on 34th street on her way to school.

_____

_____

10. Teachers are expected to *pore over* their students' papers, so they can give a thorough feedback on how well they are doing with their homework and tests.

_____

_____

11. Charles has wrongly *interpreted* Miyuki's action.

_____

_____

THE PROCESS OF MAKING SPEECH

Reading through interviews about *coping* with stage fright, there seems to be a common denominator among all of them.

N Pair Work: **Answer the following questions with your partner.**

1. Choose two topics that you would like to talk about:

a. _____

b. _____

2. Why did you choose such topics?

3. Are you comfortable talking about controversial issues? In what venues?

4. Do you think your audience would be interested in listening to you?

5. How will you gather your information to develop a topic?

1. TIPS ON CHOOSING YOUR TOPIC

- The topic should cover a wide range, but for first time presenters, try to start off with topics that you are most familiar with. This way, developing your speech will not be a *struggle*. Talking about something familiar will definitely be *a breeze*.

- Choose a topic that will not be difficult to develop, and is interesting to you, even if you know little or nothing about it. While you will have to undertake some research to develop a speech that is interesting to you, at least the work will not be so *burdensome*.

- Start off by noting down some general topics that are either familiar or interesting to you. It could be about: places in your country that you are proud of and would like your class to know about, it could be your favorite sport and why you like it so much, it could be about a recent experience that you had when you came to the United States to study English.

On the other hand, interesting topics could be why most of the streets of New York are named with numbers instead of people's names which is different from other countries; it could be the rise to power and fame of President Barack Obama, or it could be about the life of a celebrity whom you are a fan of.

You will notice that these topics are all very general. This is all right. However, your topic may be so general that your speech presentation will end up being too long. So the second step that you should do is to focus on a particular aspect of that topic and develop your speech presentation based on that. For example, if you want to talk about a recent experience, of which you must have had a lot since you arrived, you could focus on one that had an impact on you because of your culture. For example, here in the United States, particularly in big cities like New York, when taking the elevator, people always stand on the right side and pass on the left. In other countries, this *convention* may not be followed.

If you want an interesting topic, make sure that you focus on an interesting aspect of the general topic. For example, political *analysts* say that President Obama's reelection was *fueled* largely by votes coming from the youth sector of the electorate. Why do you think he appealed more to them than did Gov. Mitt Romney? Focusing on this aspect of President Obama's reelection would be more manageable than speaking in general terms about his rise to political *preeminence*.

2. RESEARCHING YOUR TOPIC

Speaking about a topic about which you have *first-hand* knowledge needs research, too. You have to research within yourself and outside of yourself to discover details about this topic. In the example of the comparison between riding escalators in New York City and your home city, you may want to interview ten New Yorkers to see if they follow this convention.

On the other hand, to derive information about the youth vote that helped the reelection of President Obama, you would have to do more *intensive* research. For such a topic, newspapers would be a good source of information. With technology being so advanced and available, researching has become less difficult. It is recommended that you tap primary sources, such as research-specific websites or newspaper websites. The New York Public Library has free Internet services and has a full staff that will help guide your research. While Wikipedia has become very popular, the data available on this website is not 100% *irrefutable*.

3. PRACTICE!!! PRACTICE!!! PRACTICE!!!

You've taken the trouble of choosing your topic wisely, focusing on its most important aspect, researching details about it, and even coming up with *compelling* visual aids for your final presentation. You are also equipped with the tools necessary to make your presentation compelling. Don't stop there! Practice your presentation before you finally face your audience. You don't want all of your efforts to *go to waste* with a poor delivery.

The best way to practice, of course, is in front of an audience. If you have supportive friends or family, this would not be difficult. Family and friends would always have time to spare to listen to you and give you constructive criticism. They could give you feedback on what is good and what is not in your presentation. Moreover, you could not have a better audience because they can be honest without making you feel insecure, and based on their critique and based on this, make *modifications* in your presentation.

What if you have no family and friends to help you practice your presentation? Should you just do it without practicing and just do your presentation on the fly? There is another option, which is, to deliver your presentation in front of a full-length mirror. Does this sound too strange and weird? And uncomfortable?

Not exactly. This technique is a popular one among actors. In fact, some speakers rely on this method BEFORE trying out their presentation in front of family and friends. After all, speaking in front of a mirror gives you a clear picture of yourself: how you speak, how you stand, how you gesture.

An *adjunct* to this technique is to take a video of yourself while rehearsing your speech. This is far better than speaking to yourself before a mirror because watching the playback will show you a better image of how well you have delivered your speech. Taking a self-video is no longer difficult or expensive, as smart-phones have become commonplace and popular.

📖 VOCABULARY IN CONTEXT   V W

🔘 Read the following sentences and use contextual clues to write the meaning of the boldfaced words.

1. When Maria arrived in Seoul, she had two suitcases, a purse and a computer bag, so it was quite a ***struggle*** for her to manage all of her luggage.

_____

_____

2. On the other hand, Won Seok only had a small suitcase and a backpack, and getting out of the airport was ***a breeze***.

_____

_____

3. Jonas said that he can't imagine life without his iPad, especially because all of his textbooks have been converted into ebooks. Having to carry real books to school every day would be just too ***burdensome***.

_____

_____

4. Gerard hardly follows the norm and ignores ***convention*** when it comes to choosing his clothes, which is why he always looks unique.

_____

_____

5. Amarinder is studying to become a climate change *analyst* so he can examine weather data and interpret these for use in an international database.

_____

_____

6. Monica's Christmas presents of brand-name clothes *fueled* her to go on a crash diet.

_____

_____

7. The *preeminence* of the iPhone comes with a price because it is so entertaining to use, people have become more distracted and less connected.

_____

_____

8. Randy gave a riveting *first-hand* account of his first sky-diving experience.

_____

_____

9. Nina underwent an *intensive* diet and exercise program so she would lose the 20 pounds that she had gained over the past year.

_____

_____

10. Gilbert provided ***irrefutable*** proof that convinced everybody that indeed, the Loch Ness Monster is just a myth.

_____

_____

_____

11. Katherine was ***compelled*** to transfer to the University to finish her Bachelor's degree.

_____

_____

12. Tony and Jackie never let anything in their house ***go to waste*** because they are such avid environmentalists.

_____

_____

13. Mike has made so many ***modifications*** to his car that it no longer looks like an old second-hand car.

_____

_____

14. Jennifer was not happy that besides having to write a term paper, her professor gave an ***adjunct*** requirement that would probably take a week to complete.

_____

_____

HELPFUL COMMONLY-USED WORDS AND PHRASES

In most public speaking activities, there are words and phrases that are commonly used by seasoned speakers. It would be helpful to learn these.

The following list is by no means exclusive, and we will learn more of these along the way.

1. Greetings or salutations–it is not only polite, but it is also customary to greet your audience before you begin your speech. A greeting of *"good morning"* or *"hello"* is a good way to establish an initial bond with your listeners.

2. Throughout your speech, be polite to your listeners. As in any setting involving social interaction, do not forget your manners. You could say, *"Please allow me to present my position on this issue,"* or *"I would like to…,"* *"If I may…,"* and other similar phrases to show that you are asking your audience for their indulgence or permission to share your views with them.

3. As you begin your speech with a greeting, you should also end it with a farewell word or phrase, and do not forget to thank your audience. You could say, *"This wraps up my presentation today, and I wish you all a good day. Thank you."*

Aa PRONUNCIATION DRILLS & GLOSSARY

See Teacher's Manual

P Do Listen & Repeat (L/R) and Choral Intonation Practice of the vocabulary words and phrases in the order in which they were presented in the book. Listen to the teacher, and put the stress marks on the words.

VOCABULARY WORD	PART OF SPEECH	PRONUNCIATION	DEFINITION
a breeze	adjective (always used in the singular form)	ey breez	easy
adjunct	adjective	**aj**-uhngkt	additional
altogether	adverb	awl-tuh-**geth**-er	completely
analyst	noun	**an**-l-ist	someone who examines or analyzes
assure	verb	uh-**shur**	guarantee the truth of something
audition	verb	aw-**dish**-uhn	to try out for a role in a play, or for a musical gig
bear in mind	phrasal verb	bair in mahynd	remember, take note
behemoth	noun	bih-**hee**-muhth	someone powerful or influential
bespectacled	adjective	bih-**spek**-tuh-kuhld	wearing eyeglasses
blunder	noun	**bluhn**-der	mistake
bone up on	phrasal verb, idiom	bohn uhp awn	to study further, review
burdensome	adjective	**bur**-dn-suhm	difficult
chief	adjective	cheef	main, principal

common denominator	noun	**kom**-uhn dih-**nom**-uh-ney-ter	a characteristic or quality or trait that could collectively describe a group
compel	verb	kuhm-**pel**	to force someone
confide	verb	kuhn-**fahyd**	tell something in confidence
convention	noun	kuhn-**ven**-shuhn	rule
cope	verb	kohp	deal with, handle
daily grind	noun	dey-lee grahynd	monotonous daily routine
debilitating	adjective	dih-**bil**-i-teytin	weakening
down pat	adjective	doun pat	understood completely
first-hand	adjective	furst hand	personal
flawless	adjective	**flaw**-lis	without a blemish, perfect
fuel	verb	**fyoo**-uhl	to make something happen
gaffe	noun	gaf	an obvious mistake
gauge	verb	geyj	measure
go south	phrasal verb	goh south	decline
go to waste	verb	goh too weyst	to leave unutilized or wasted
guts	noun (always in the plural form)	guhts	courage
haphazard	adjective	hap-haz-erd	without a plan or specific direction, careless
inappropriate	adjective	in-uh-proh-pree-it	not proper
insecurity	noun	in-si-kyoor-i-tee	the feeling of being inferior or unsure
intensive	adjective	in-ten-siv	serious, intense
interpret	verb	in-tur-prit	to explain from one's own point of view

iota	noun	ahy-oh-tuh	a very small quantity
irrefutable	adjective	ih-ref-yuh-tuh-buhl	cannot be disputed
jovial	adjective	joh-vee-uhl	good-natured
lenient	adjective	lee-nee-uhnt	not strict
manifest	verb	man-uh-fest	show
mindful	adjective	mahynd-fuhl	aware
modification	noun	mod-uh-fi-key-shuhn	change
mouthful	adjective	mouth-fool	a word or sentence that is long and difficult to say
muffled	adjective	muhf-uhl	dull-sounding
not to mention	adverb	not too men-shuhn	much less
off	adjective	awf	not right
ophthalmology	noun	of-thal-mo-lo-jee	the medical science that studies the eye
over-compensation	noun	oh-ver kom-puhn-sey-shuhn	an attempt to hide an unacceptable trait by doing something its opposite
pocket change	noun	pok-it cheynj	insignificant amount of money
pore over	phrasal verb	pawr-oh-ver	to examine or study carefully
preeminence	noun	pree-em-uh-nuhns	being important or popular
primed	verb	prahymd	got ready
qualms	noun	kwahms	misgivings, second thoughts
raucous	adjective	raw-kuhs	noisy, loud
retch	noun	rech	feel as vomiting
root cause	noun	root keys	primary or main reason
rule of thumb	noun	rool ov thuhm	guess, estimate
scrawny	adjective	skraw-nee	skinny

scrutiny	noun	skroot-n-ee	inspection
seasoned	adjective	see-zuhnd	highly experienced
sheepish	adjective	shee-pish	shy
stature	noun	stach-er	height, reputation
stodgy	adjective	stoj-ee	boring
struggle	noun	struhg-uh	challenge
subject one's self to (something)	idiom	suhb-jekt-wuhn-self-too-suhm-thing	make one's self go through something, usually unpleasant or unwelcome
succumb	verb	suh-kuhm	~~order~~ to give in
telegraph	verb	tel-i-graf	show, to make your audience aware of your mistakes or fear of facing them
to get butterflies in one's stomach	verb	too get-buht-er-flahy in wuhns-stuhm-uhk	to be nervous
to give someone the jitters	phrasal verb, idiom	too giv -suhm-wuhn th ee-jit-ers	to make someone nervous
to have a sense of	verb	too huhv ey sens ov	to have a feeling or an idea of something
to make a beeline for	phrasal verb, idiom	too meyk ey bee-lahyn fawr	to eagerly approach someone, or to excitedly line up for something
to say the least	adverb	too sey th ee leest	without exaggerating
trauma	noun	trrraw-muh	the emotional result of an unforgettable experience (usually with a negative connotation)
trick	noun	trik	technique
unnerving	adjective	uhn-nurvin	intimidating
vice versa	adjective	vahys-versa	applicable both ways

Unit 2

PUBLIC SPEAKING

"What we say is important, for in most cases the mouth speaks what the heart is full of."

Jim Beggs

WARM UP ACTIVITY

A Group Work: In groups of three, list five (5) things that came to your mind and why you chose them: your favorite food, the latest movies you have seen, your movie idols, your favorite sports, etc. Choose a leader to write the group's responses.

1. _____

2. _____

3. _____

4. _____

5. _____

B Group Work/Jigsaw:
Share your group's responses to other groups.

_____

_____

_____

_____

_____

_____

WHAT IS PUBLIC SPEAKING?

Now that we've dealt with the ***preliminaries*** of stage fright, let's get to the meat of the matter: What is public speaking? Believe it or not, public speaking–in its broadest sense–is ***prevalent*** in our daily lives.

The general ***notion*** is that public speaking is when you make a presentation before an audience. Do you agree or disagree? However, did you know that what we just did, which was to ask each other questions and share our opinions in class, is considered public speaking? Even asking a stranger on the street a question about directions or general information, which most of us have done at one point or another, is also public speaking.

Do you agree, or disagree?

Of these three forms of public speaking, the first is the most common ***conception*** of what public speaking is, and the source of that unseen enemy, stage fright.

Communication is one of the most fundamental tools that every human being possesses. Speech communication **sets us apart** from other animals, and it is through language that we are able to exchange ideas with others, and let others understand what we want or feel.

While there are some who have a good background in making public presentations, others do not. It is therefore the objective of this book to help all of those who wish to make a better and more effective public presentation, by planning, creating and delivering a speech before an audience.

HOW TO PLAN A SPEECH PRESENTATION?

Preparing a speech or presentation is not as difficult as it seems. You may have taken a writing class previously, and may have learned about the many genres of writing, and more essentially, how to write effectively. Planning a speech presentation is not as difficult as it seems. All you need to remember is to structure your speech the way you would a written exercise, namely, it must have these three important parts:

- Introduction
- Body
- Conclusion

If you remember your previous writing classes, you will recall that *on paper,* these three parts will appear in this order. However, most writers prepare their speech by writing the body first. Why is this? This is because the body contains the most important parts of the presentation, and it is from the body that you are able to express your introduction and conclusion. It is the body that gives form to your presentation and contains the most important parts of your speech. The introduction gives a *glimpse* of your presentation and offers your audience a peek at what you will be talking about, and the conclusion wraps up and encapsulates what you have just discussed.

On the other hand, other writers choose to write the conclusion first. Wait. This seems *counter-intuitive* and *downright* wrong. After all, our previous lessons emphasize that the conclusion contains the summary and restatement of the introduction, so how can the conclusion be developed first? Well, it is precisely because of this that some writers feel comfortable writing the conclusion first, because then they can develop the speech backwards. To them, the conclusion provides a *snapshot* of how the entire speech is going to look like. Based on this snapshot, the details of the body can then be developed.

IT ALL DEPENDS ON YOU!

Which is the correct way to write your speech, then? Well, it all depends on you! Try different *approaches*, and see for yourself which one works best for you.

We have discussed stage fright, and we have discussed structure; now let's start learning how to speak!

VOCABULARY IN CONTEXT

C Read the following sentences and use contextual clues to write the meaning of the boldfaced words, then create your own sentence using the same vocabulary word supplied in the exercise.

1. Stacey needed to complete the *preliminaries* of her major at her university before she was allowed to enroll in the next course.

Meaning: _____

Sentence: _____

2. Because many of his classmates have the flu, Joshua believes that it has become *prevalent* this winter season.

Meaning: _____

Sentence: _____

3. Juancho's *notion* of a good ESL class is one that combines grammar, writing, speaking and writing.

Meaning: _____

Sentence: _____

4. Choi *overcame* the *conception* that all hamburgers taste the same after he tried the ones at Shake Shack.

Meaning: _____

_____

Sentence: _____

5. Gabriel *sets* himself *apart* from other students by coming to class in unusual outfits.

Meaning: _____

Sentence: _____

6. Anaïs did not realize learning how to bake cupcakes was so difficult. It seemed easy *on paper*, but even after following the recipe to the letter, her first attempt was disappointing.

Meaning: _____

Sentence: _____

7. Julian believes that it is *counter-intuitive* for an iPad user to ask for a manual of instructions because the iPad is supposed to be easy to use from the get-go.

Meaning: _____

Sentence: _____

8. Seeing a picture of his baby makes Andres *downright* happy.

Meaning: _____

Sentence: _____

9. Olivia always prepares an outline before writing a speech because it provides a *snapshot* of what she will be talking about.

Meaning: _____

Sentence: _____

10. Overcoming stage fright can be done through many *approaches*, but to Elsa, the best approach is still practice, practice, practice.

Meaning: _____

Sentence: _____

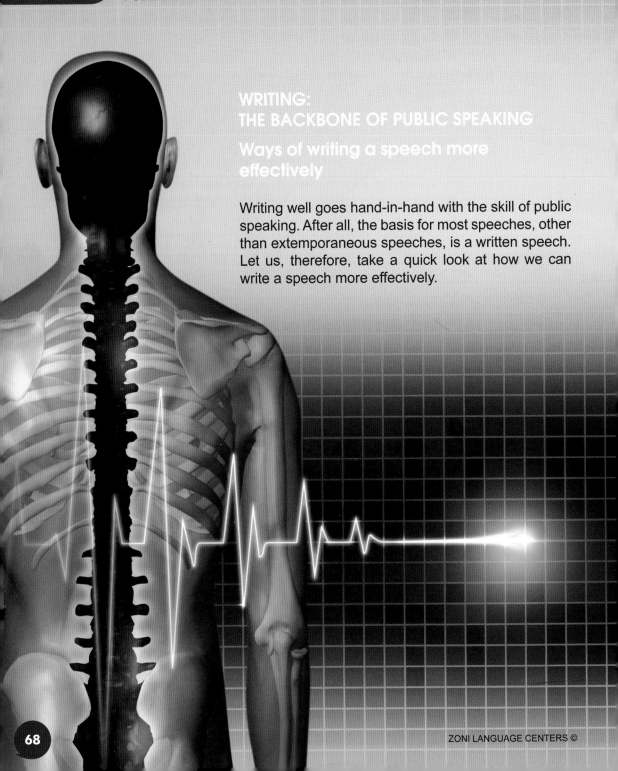

WRITING:
THE BACKBONE OF PUBLIC SPEAKING

Ways of writing a speech more effectively

Writing well goes hand-in-hand with the skill of public speaking. After all, the basis for most speeches, other than extemporaneous speeches, is a written speech. Let us, therefore, take a quick look at how we can write a speech more effectively.

1. | IDENTIFYING THE TOPIC OF YOUR SPEECH

A good way to start your speech is by writing down the ideas that will go into your speech, from the general to the specific. Let's say, for example, that you would like to talk about pets, but talking about pets is general. Which kind of pet would you like to talk about? You could choose dogs. But there are many types of dogs, classified by breed, one of which, is the pug. Now why would you like to take care of a pug? Perhaps you are a single person and need a "housemate." Now, you have narrowed down the specific topic that you are going to talk about.

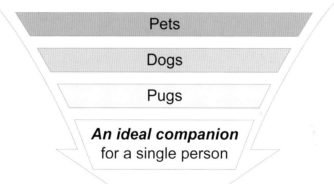

Pets

Dogs

Pugs

An ideal companion
for a single person

Doing this pre-writing activity will help you develop your topic better. You could use this technique in organizing even an extemporaneous speech, by imagining in your mind the specifics of what you want to talk about at a given moment.

2. DEVELOPING YOUR TOPIC SENTENCE

The topic sentence not only introduces your paragraph or speech, it also encapsulates the controlling idea of your topic. It is called the controlling idea for good reason: your topic sentence will dictate how the rest of the sentences in your paragraph will be developed.

[Example]   Controlling Idea

Topic sentence: A pug is an ideal companion for a single person.

The controlling idea is that a pug is **an ideal companion**. The rest of your paragraph or speech should therefore show why this is so.

D Pair Work: **With a partner identify the topic (by underlining it once), and the controlling idea (by underlining it twice), in each of the following topic sentences.**

1. Working part-time is bad for my studies.

2. The subway system of New York City needs immediate rennovation.

3. Attack dogs, like the Doberman or pit bull, should not be kept as pets.

4. You can never rely on the Internet to meet new friends.

5. Why ice cream is good for you in winter and bad for you in summer.

3. REFINING YOUR TOPIC SENTENCE FURTHER

Sometimes, we come across a speech that is so badly-written, and part of the reason for this is probably because the topic sentence was not written in a more specific or focused way.

[Example] Topic sentence: A pug is an ideal companion for a single person.

This topic sentence could still be refined. Why is a pug ideal as a companion for someone who is single? Is it because a pug in itself has some special qualities that improve a person's life? Since there still appears some vagueness in this topic sentence, it needs to be improved further.

[Example] Improved topic sentence:

Research has shown that owning and taking care of a pug results in health benefits for a single person.

Here, the source of the idea of why having a pug is identified. Additionally, the acts that would result in health benefits, namely owning and taking care of a pug, are clearly stated. Next, the result of taking care of a pug, which is health benefits, is also mentioned. This refinement of the topic sentence makes it much clearer than the original one.

Pair Practice

E Pair Work: **With a partner, improve the topic sentence in Exercise D (page 70).**

1. _____

2. _____

3. _____

4. _____

5. _____

4. FORMULATING YOUR SUPPORTING SENTENCES

A paragraph needs to be cohesive and fully-developed. To this end, the speaker must provide supporting sentences to help his/her audience fully appreciate his/her speech.

[Example]

Topic sentence:

Research has shown that owning and taking care of a pug results in health benefits for a single person.

Supporting sentences:

a. The single lifestyle has been shown to shorten life expectancy in men and women.

b. Some singles live in small apartments, preventing them from owning a big dog.

c. However, a toy dog, like the pug, is usually allowed in most apartments. The pug is easy to train, does not bark, and is still mobile.

d. Single persons should, therefore, try to own a pug.

e. Singles with pugs go to the doctor less often and live longer.

F Group Work: **In groups of three, work on** Exercise E **(page 71), and expand one of the topics by coming up with sentences that support the topic sentence.**

_____

_____

_____

_____

5. MAKING YOUR SPEECH INTERESTING TO YOUR AUDIENCE

a. Begin your speech with a HOOK (attention-getter)

An effective speech needs to be more than just well-written. A cohesive speech, or one that follows the rule of structure and organization, will not be necessarily one that will capture the attention of your audience or hold them *captive*. A good speech must start with a line or an idea that will make your audience sit up and pay attention to what you are saying. Without this "hook," you will lose the interest of your listeners. A great example of this is the historic *"I Have A Dream"* speech delivered by the Rev. Martin Luther King, Jr. at the foot of the Lincoln Memorial in Washington, D.C. on August 28, 1963. The speech began with the line, ***"I am happy to join with you today in what will go down in history as the greatest demonstration for freedom in the history of our nation."*** While this opening line drew *hearty* applause from the *multitude* of men and women who watched him, Rev. King was not able to hold their attention. It was only towards the latter part of the speech, when he spoke of the dreams that he had, that the audience truly connected with him. The hook came later in the speech; nonetheless, it was a very effective hook.

*You can read the full speech at
http://www.archives.gov/press/exhibits/dream-speech.pdf

b. Make your speech RELEVANT

The speaker connects to his audience when he speaks about something relevant. Rev. King would not have been as captivating on the day that he delivered his speech, if he had spoken about gardening, would he? Making speech relevant is part of a speaker's preparation. Besides knowing in advance what to talk about, the speaker must find out who he/she will be speaking for: gender, age and other information on an audience's background are important in fine-tuning a speech.

G Teamwork: **Elicit from your team famous hooks in speeches your team have come across or heard, and let them identify the topic, audience, occasion.**

[Example]

Basic information:

Audience: Graduating class, College graduates

Topic: Challenges in a Competitive World

Hook (Attention getter): What is your competitive advantage, now that you are graduates? Are you ready to face the job market?

c. Establish your CREDIBILITY

Have you ever been to an event with a speaker who failed because he/she was not believable? I remember one occasion where the audience was made up mostly of established businessmen and the speaker was supposed to have been an expert on the stock market. Unfortunately, the speaker had to cancel at the last minute, and sent an assistant to read his speech. It was, expectedly, a disaster. It was *akin* to having a child lecture his father on how to raise children. Not everyone is an expert, but a speaker should thoroughly research his/her topic beforehand so that he/she is able to establish his/her credibility and answer any questions that are raised by his/her audience.

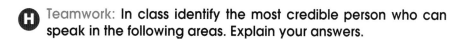

H Teamwork: **In class identify the most credible person who can speak in the following areas. Explain your answers.**

1. Health

2. Politics & Government

3. Sports

4. Education

5. Environment

WHAT IS INFORMATIVE SPEECH?

Information is the key to success in the world today. The following three examples illustrate the importance of information in our daily lives. A stock broker scans newspapers, business financial statements and annual reports to make decisions that will make money for his/her clients. A doctor reads medical journals, vital charts and patient information to find the best diagnosis and treatment for their patients. An advertising executive uses information to develop ideas and brands that will appeal to a targeted segment of the population. All of these people have in common the importance of information in order to do their jobs.

When we write informative speeches our main tasks are to research, organize and present information as clearly and interestingly as possible. Imagine that you are the teacher and you are providing information that you feel is important for your students' success. The purpose of your speech should be to provide interesting, useful and unique information. Informative speeches can be about almost anything as long as you think it is important and relevant to the listeners.

1 Answer the following questions and if you don't know the answer leave it blank until you can ask another classmate. After you have asked students in the class go to the Internet room and research the answers to the questions you don't have an answer for. Then discuss the information that you have researched.

1. What is big data?
2. How did the dinosaurs become extinct?
3. How do you play American football?
4. How was the English language formed?
5. How does a law get made and passed in the United States Federal Government?

PRESENTATION ACTIVITY

See Teacher's Manual

In this part of the book, we will be reading about a very important issue: juvenile delinquency. Each paragraph has a topic and supporting sentences. Let us see if we can identify the topic sentence and supporting sentences in each paragraph, and see how the topic sentence was developed. Does the speech contain a hook? Is it relevant, and how is the speaker's credibility established in the speech?

Example "Informative Speech"

The Rising Problem Of Juvenile Delinquency*

On October 20, 2012, a 14 year-old girl, Autumn Pasquale, went missing in Clayton, N.J. She was last seen riding her white BMX bike. The police and volunteers launched a massive *manhunt*, and on Monday, October 22, 2012, her body was found inside a recycling bin, and the cause of death was *blunt force trauma*. The mother of two teenage boys, 15-year-old Justin Robinson and 17-year-old Dante, alerted the police after seeing a suspicious message on one of the two boys' Facebook account. The boys' mother allowed the police into her home to investigate, where they recovered the girl's bike and backpack. The two boys were known to be BMX bike *aficionados*, and they *lured* Autumn into their house to sell bike accessories to her. The boys were charged for the murder as adults, instead of being brought under the *juvenile justice system*.

*Research culled from
www.wikipedia.org and www.cbsnews.com

The Robinson case highlights the growing problem of juvenile delinquency in the United States, where more than 70 million or 25 percent of the population is comprised of children under the age of 18. This number is expected to exceed 80 million by the year 2020. These numbers suggest the serious nature and multitude of issues affecting children in the United States, particularly children who are at risk of falling into the juvenile justice system.

What is juvenile delinquency? This is loosely defined as the participation in illegal behavior by an individual younger than the age of majority, typically under the age of 18. Such a delinquent would have been charged with a crime, if he had been an adult. Still, the juvenile justice system has made it possible for persons under 18 to be charged and tried as adults, depending on the type and seriousness of the crime committed.

Juvenile delinquents are mostly young men. It is believed that young men are more likely to commit illegal acts because of the pressures that they undergo as teenagers to be tough and aggressive, and this behavior becomes a way for them to express and assert their *masculinity*. Acting out their masculinity could make young men more likely to engage in criminal behavior.

Race is another factor in this issue. This could be because most juvenile offenders come from low-income households, which in turn have been found to have parents who either are too lenient or too harsh with their children, and where associating with *deviant* peer groups is prevalent. Additionally, the majority of adolescents who live in low-income households are racial minorities, and minorities who commit crimes or any act deemed offensive, even as adolescents, are more likely to be arrested and punished more harshly by the law if caught. However, while poor minorities are more likely to commit violent crimes, reports have also shown that 1/3 of affluent adolescents commit violent crimes.

Cause Of Juvenile Delinquency

Criminologists and social scientists have *theorized* on why the phenomenon of juvenile delinquency exists. Among the causes that they have identified are the following:

1. Children who perform poorly at school are also more likely to be *truant*, and *truancy* is linked to criminal offenses. *Impulsiveness* is seen by some as the key aspect of a child's upbringing that predicts juvenile delinquency.

2. Children brought up by a stepparent are more likely to start offending than those who live with two natural parents. It is also more likely that children of single parents may live in poverty, which, as has been mentioned, is strongly associated with juvenile delinquency.

3. If a child has little parental supervision, they are much more likely to break the law. Many studies have found a strong correlation between a lack of supervision and criminal offenses.

4. Brothers and sisters of adolescents with criminal records are more likely to be influenced by their siblings, and also become delinquent, especially if the delinquent sibling is older, of the same sex/gender, and nurturing towards the younger sibling.

5. Rejection in childhood is also a large predictor of juvenile delinquency. Although children are rejected by peers for many reasons, it is often the case that they are rejected due to violent or aggressive behavior. This type of rejection often leads them to gravitate towards anti-social peer groups.

6. An inferior education is another factor that has been identified as having a correlation to juvenile delinquency. Children who receive little or no education have difficulty achieving wealth and status by securing well-paid employment, and are therefore more likely to use crime as a means to obtain both money and status.

7. Labeling a child early on as a criminal increases the likelihood of he/she becoming one. A child who is labeled as deviant may accept that label, and

will act out that role. This in turn will lead him to associate with others who have been similarly labeled. Research indicates that male children from poor families are more likely to be labeled deviant, and this may partially explain why there are more young male offenders.

8. Mental and behavioral disorders also contribute to juvenile delinquency. Psychopaths are often diagnosed with aggressive and antisocial personality disorders, which can develop during childhood and later manifest during adolescence.

Can Juvenile Delinquency Be Prevented?

This is a question that has become controversial and **contentious**. Juvenile delinquency has many causes, and for it to be prevented, the approach to its prevention must be broad and comprehensive. Each of the aforementioned causes should be addressed. Counseling, both of parents and children, seems like a good starting point towards this goal. Moreover, children identified as prone to delinquency must be monitored, and the causes contributing to their delinquency must be removed. In some cases, removing a child from a risk-prone environment may even be necessary. Still, there have also been studies showing that often, attempting to prevent delinquency may make things worse for **risk-prone children**. This could be because placing large groups of risk-prone children together only encourages delinquent or violent behavior. When "bad" teens get together to talk about the "bad" things they've done, it is received by their peers in a positive reinforcing light, and this promoted juvenile behavior among them. It is believed that the most efficient **interventions** are those that not only separate at-risk teens from anti-social peers, and place them instead with pro-social ones, but also simultaneously improve their home environment by training parents with appropriate parenting styles. It is hoped that such a comprehensive approach will successfully reform risk-prone children. There have been successful cases of juvenile reform, but they took a lot of effort and time to complete.

Could the murder of the 14 year-old girl have been prevented? Her alleged murderers appear to fit a lot of the causes of juvenile delinquency: Dante and Justin are black, raised in a poor racial background, and it is possible that Dante was nurturing towards his younger brother, Justin. Did their mother detect their risk-prone behavior earlier on but did nothing about it? Who knows? Perhaps if a deeper study were made on their case, more data could have been gathered to ascertain if they could have been helped, before they acted on their criminal tendencies.

❓ COMPREHENSION QUESTIONS

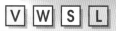
V W S L

J Group Work: **Work in groups of five and identify the following components of the article.**

1. Hook (attention getter)
2. Thesis
3. Topic sentence and supporting sentences in each paragraph
4. Conclusion

K Group Work: **Discuss the following questions.**

1. What is the relevance of this topic?
2. How can you detect the credibility of the writer/speaker?

CLASS ACTIVITY

 Group Work: **As a class develop a speech topic whose presentation would be greatly enhanced with visual aids: for example, PLASTIC SURGERY.**

Step 1 IDENTIFYING THE TOPIC OF YOUR SPEECH

 Using the "Ways of writing a speech more effectively 1-5", let's develop the topic.

PLASTIC SURGERY

THE PROS AND CONS OF PLASTIC SURGERY

ADDICTION TO PLASTIC SURGERY

Step 2 DEVELOPING YOUR TOPIC SENTENCE

Now that we have decided to speak about

"Addiction to plastic surgery."

Let us develop a topic sentence.

Let us say that your topic sentence is

"Addiction to plastic surgery could result in more harm than good."

Step 3 REFINING YOUR TOPIC SENTENCE FURTHER

Suggest ways by which you can further refine the topic sentence.

Let us say that the refinement you made to your topic sentence is

"Repeated plastic surgery results in unpleasant changes to the patient's face and body, and should therefore not be allowed."

Step 4 FORMULATING YOUR SUPPORTING SENTENCES

With our topic sentence,

"Repeated plastic surgery results in unpleasant changes to the patient's face and body, and should therefore not be allowed."

Let us now come up with the sentences supporting this. There might be physical, financial, emotional and psychological effects involved, and you could provide a supporting sentence for following effects.

a. Repeated surgeries expose the patient to long-term risks of infections, scarring, hemorrhages, organ failure and all other risks associated with surgeries (PHYSICAL).

b. Most plastic surgery patients have a distorted body image of themselves and repeated surgeries will make their condition worse (PSYCHOLOGICAL).

c. Make your own supporting statement

_____

_____

_____

d. Make your own supporting statement

_____

_____

_____

Step 5 MAKING YOUR SPEECH INTERESTING TO YOUR AUDIENCE

 Besides starting your speech with a HOOK to get them interested in your topic, we have also discussed adding visual aids to your presentation to make it more compelling. A topic on the negative effects of plastic surgery is well-served with the addition of images.

🌐 INTERNET ASSIGNMENTS   V W

Ⓜ Using the Internet, come up with the following research points to generate the needed visual aids for your presentation.

1. The scientific terms for the cause of addiction to plastic surgery.

2. Specific examples of plastic surgery addicts. Pictures of these addicts may be used for your presentation. It would be interesting to show before-and-after pictures to drive home the point that most of these addicts did not even require plastic surgery to begin with.

3. Why do plastic surgeons give in to the repeated demands of their patients to undergo plastic surgery? Should plastic surgeons who perform multiple surgeries on a patient be held liable for aggravating the self-esteem issues of their patients?

NOTE

Remember to always cite in your presentation the source of materials taken from the internet.

[Example]

Torres, E.C.B, (March 4, 2013). Beauty addiction, Psychology Today, 5. article 0123. Retrieved March 31, 2014, from http://www. psychology today/article/art 0123.html

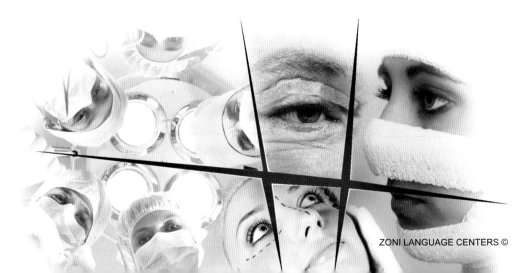

PRESENTATION ACTIVITY

Make a short presentation on the topic, *"Repeated plastic surgery results in unpleasant changes in the patient's face and body, and should therefore not be allowed,"* using the materials generated from your Internet research. Limit the presentation to a maximum of 7 minutes. The key points of your presentation should be spelled out in bullet points, and should be highlighted by visual aids, preferably using PowerPoint, that will clearly illustrate the detrimental effects of repeated plastic surgery.

HELPFUL COMMONLY-USED WORDS AND PHRASES

This Unit deals with the informative and self-introductory speeches. It would help you to learn some words and phrases commonly used in these types of speeches. As in the similar section in Unit 1, the following list is by no means exclusive, and the words and phrases listed there, are also useful in giving informative or self-introductory speeches. You will learn more of these as you develop your speech skills.

1. *"Hello, my name is…"* –among the most commonly-used greetings in the English language, if not the most commonly-used, is hello. It is universally familiar, and starting your self-introductory speech with such a well-known greeting establishes at least two things: your courtesy and your friendliness. Invariably, when a speaker says hello, his/her audience responds the same way. Hearing hellos from both the speaker and the audience immediately establishes rapport between them.

2. *"Did you ever wonder what/why/where/how…"* –one of the techniques of effective communication is to engage your audience at the very start of your speech, and a good way to do this is to ask your audience a question. This technique is especially helpful in informative speeches. Not everyone in your audience may know much about your topic, and asking them if they do will challenge them and pique their interest. In engaging your audience, you will very likely have an audience that will be attentive to your presentation.

3. *"Take for example…" "An example of…" "Another example of…"* –the ideas in an informative speech become clearer when examples are given to support these ideas. Introduce each example with phrases such as the ones above.

Aa PRONUNCIATION DRILLS & GLOSSARY

See Teacher's Manual

Do Listen & Repeat (L/R) and Choral Intonation Practice of the vocabulary words and phrases in the order in which they were presented in the book. Listen to the teacher, and put the stress marks on the words.

VOCABULARY WORD	PART OF SPEECH	PRONUNCIATION	DEFINITION
aficionados	noun	uh-fish-yuh-**nah**-dohs	enthusiast, fanatic
akin	adjective	uh-**kin**	comparable, similar
approach	noun	uh-**prohch**	method, access
blunt force trauma	noun	bluhnt-fawrs-**traw**muh	injury either by impact or attack
captive	adjective	**kap**-tiv	enslaved, confined
conception	noun	kuhn-**sep**-shuhn	notion, idea
contentious	adjective	kuhn-**ten**-shuhs	causing argument
counter-intuitive	adjective	koun-ter-in-**too**-i-tiv	against what is normally expected
deviant	adjective	dee-vee-**uhnt**	departing from the norm
downright	adjective	doun-**rahyt**	straightforward, direct
glimpse	noun	glimps	very brief look, vague idea
hearty	adjective	**hahr**-tee	warm-hearted, affectionate
impulsiveness	noun	im-**puhl**-sivnes	spontaneity, without thinking

intervention	noun	in-ter-**ven**-shuhn	getting involved in sb's affairs
juvenile justice system	noun	joo-vuh-**nl-juhs**-tis sis-tuhm	courts for crimes commited by underaged youngsters
lure	noun/verb	loor	to attract/attraction
manhunt	noun	**man**-huhnt	intensive search for a person
masculinity	noun	mas-kyuh-**liniti**	having the qualities of a man
multitude	noun	**muhl**-ti-tood	a great number of
notion	noun	**now**-shun	idea, concept
on paper	adverb	on **pay**-per	theoretically, in theory
preliminaries	noun	pree-li-mi-**na**-rees	basic principles
prevalent	adjective	**preh**-va-lent	generally accepted
risk-prone children	noun	rysk-prohn-childruyn	children who are vulnerable to taking risks
set (someone) apart	phrasal verb	set (x) a-part	to make someone noticed
snapshot	noun	snap-shot	summary
theorized	adjective	**thee**-uh-rahyzd	forming a theory
truant	noun/ adjective	**troo**-uhnt	a student who skips classes
truancy	noun	**troo**-uhn-see	the act of skipping classes

ZONI LANGUAGE CENTERS ©

Unit 3

PERSUASIVE SPEECH

" Speech is power: speech is to persuade,
to convert, to compel."

Ralph Waldo Emerson

WHAT IS PERSUASIVE SPEECH?

Persuasion is the process of convincing someone or influencing the opinion, attitude, or beliefs of others. It is done through the presentation of facts and arguments that influence the people who hear you. It is easier to understand what persuasion is by comparing it to an informative speech and noting the differences.

PRESENTATION ACTIVITY

Example "Persuasive Speech"

Medical Marijuana

Introduction:

The modern Medical Marijuana Movement began in 1972 when the drug was labeled as a controlled substance due primarily to the common thought that it had no acceptable medical use. Since then there have been many studies that suggest otherwise and *cast doubt* on the idea that marijuana is a useless drug with no medical benefits. Recently state politicians under intense pressure from *constituents* have voted and legalized medicinal marijuana use. Today, many states in the USA such as California and Colorado have legalized marijuana for medicinal use, and the trend seems to be *catching on*. In a speech by Hillary Rodham Clinton she expressed the following opinion;

"With respect to medical marijuana, you know I think that we have had a lot of *rhetoric* and the federal government has been very *intent* upon trying to prevent states from being able to offer that as an option for people who are in pain. I think we should be doing medical research on this. We ought to find out what the elements exist in marijuana that might help people who are suffering from cancer and nausea-related treatments."

Governments and citizens *stand divided* on the issue of legalizing the use of medical marijuana. There are two varying opinions; medical marijuana is an excuse for people to buy and sell drugs without being held accountable. *Medical marijuana is a part of a doctor's prescribed treatment that can be very effective and helpful for a certain group of patients*. There are two points that make the *latter* the most sensible and *viable* option.

Supporting sentences (Point 1):

Medical marijuana is the dried mixture of the leaf, flower, stem and seed of the Cannabis Sativa plant. Throughout history the marijuana plant has been widely used as a medicine, source of entertainment and as a part of cultural and religious traditions and folklore. Studies and current research being done have found some very interesting trends about the benefits of medical marijuana. Smoking marijuana has been shown to fight off the spread of certain forms of cancer cells, glaucoma, seizures, *Tourette's syndrome*, some forms of depression, hepatitis C, arthritis, diabetes, muscular sclerosis, migraine headaches, nausea and Alzheimer's disease. Medical marijuana has many of the benefits of a *wide range* of prescription drugs without their dangerous side effects.

Supporting sentences:

If medical marijuana were legal then it would be taxed and that revenue would be used by the government. It would be a *tremendous* boost to the national state, and local economies. In states where medical marijuana is already legal, revenues of between 500 million to 1 billion dollars are generating new economic opportunities and growth. Medical marijuana would also make the buying, use and selling of marijuana safer, and would effectively put the drug dealers out of business, thereby improving our communities.

Conclusion:

In conclusion, There is *resounding* evidence that suggests that the legalization of medical marijuana would be an important step in making more treatment options available and would have a large positive economic stimulus on the local and national economies. This is why medical marijuana should be legalized.

❓ COMPREHENSION QUESTIONS   S

Pair Practice

A Pair Work: **Fill out the following sentences with your opinion.**

1. When did the modern Medical Marijuana Movement begin?
2. Why was marijuana made illegal?
3. What is a controlled substance?
4. What is Hillary Clinton's position on medical marijuana?
5. What are the two varying opinions on medical marijuana?
6. Which opinion do you support and why?
7. Why is medical marijuana considered better than prescription drugs?
8. How can medical marijuana help government revenue?
9. How will legalizing medical marijuana make communities safer?
10. Does the speech support legalizing medical marijuana? If yes, why?
11. How is marijuana perceived in your native countries? Is there a movement to legalize it for medical purposes?

VOCABULARY IN CONTEXT

B Match the vocabulary word to a synonym. Use the context of the sentence to find the best match.

1. There have been many studies that suggest otherwise and ***cast doubt on*** the idea that marijuana is a useless drug with no medical benefits.

Cast doubt on is closest in meaning to:

A: hide
B: illuminate
C: question
D: find

2. Recently, state politicians under intense pressure from ***constituents***, have voted to legalize medicinal marijuana use.

Constituents is closest in meaning to:

A: manuscript
B: people
C: citizens
D: laws

3. Today, many states in the USA have legalized marijuana for medicinal use, and the trend seems to be ***catching on***.

Catching on is closest in meaning to:

A: Following a trend
B: Difficulty
C: Hard to find
D: Unimaginable

4. With respect to medical marijuana, you know, I think that we have had a lot of *rhetoric* and the federal government has been very *intent* upon trying to prevent states from being able to offer that as an option for people who are in pain.

Rhetoric is closest in meaning to:

A: confused
B: unclear
C: articulate
D: insincere promises

Intent is closest in meaning to:

A: aim
B: crowded
C: unfair
D: after

5. Governments and citizens *stand divided* on the issue of legalizing the use of medical marijuana.

Stand Divided is closest in meaning to:

A: can not agree
B: unity
C: unchangeable
D: no reason to do

6. There are two points that make the *latter* the most sensible and *viable* option.

Latter is closest in meaning to:

A: being the second of two
B: the one that comes before
C: the third one of something
D: the first one

Viable is closest in meaning to:

A: best
B: necessary
C: only
D: can be done

7. Smoking marijuana has been shown to fight off the spread of certain forms of cancer cells, glaucoma, seizures, *Tourette's syndrome*, some forms of depression, hepatitis C, arthritis, diabetes, muscular sclerosis, migraine headaches, nausea and Alzheimer's disease.

Tourette's syndrome is closest in meaning to:

A: feeling
B: initiation
C: way of life
D: a type of disease

8. Medical marijuana has many of the benefits of a **wide range** of prescription drugs without the danger of side effects.

Wide range is closest in meaning to:

A: diverse
B: homogeneous
C: important
D: lost

9. It would be a **tremendous** boost to the national and local economies.

Tremendous boost is closest in meaning to:

A: very large amount
B: large amount
C: average
D: a little

WARM UP ACTIVITY   W

C Fill out the following sentences with your opinion.

1. The best restaurant in _____ is _____ .

Because _____

_____ .

2. The city that has the most famous style is _____ .

Because _____

_____ .

3. The best kind of movie is _____ .

Because _____

_____ .

4. The best band or singer in the world is _____ .

Because _____

_____ .

5. The best thing about the country that I am studying English in is

_____ .

Because _____

_____ .

6. The healthiest food is _____.

Because _____

_____ .

7. The worst kind of weather to live in is _____ .

Because _____

_____   _____ .

8. The easiest part about learning a new language is _____ .

Because _____   _____

_____ .

9. The most difficult thing about living in a new country is

_____

_____ .

Because _____

_____ .

10. The most beautiful/handsome person in the world is

_____ .

Because _____

_____ .

FOUR STEPS TO CREATE A PERSUASIVE SPEECH

When you are creating a persuasive speech you must follow a logical step of four processes that are essential to delivering a convincing persuasive speech. How you manage the information you will present is the most important aspect of persuasive speech writing and execution. Many speeches have started out with a lot of enthusiasm and interest in the topic but end up mired due to inefficient planning and research. The following sections provide you with a ***strong foundation*** in the four step process of creating a persuasive speech.

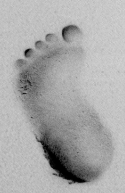

1. FINDING A TOPIC

When you are preparing a topic for persuasive speech, remember that it should be a topic that is fun and interesting. Try to choose a topic that you find personally important or *moved by*. Do not choose a topic just because it is easy to write and present. In a persuasive speech you must have an opinion that will convince someone of your point of view.

D Group Work: **Work in groups and rate the following topics in order of your interest from 1-10 make sure to add 2 more topics that you want to speak about to the list. Compare your answers with other classmates.**

1. _____ Make up is important, if you want to be beautiful.

2. _____ Hip Hop is the most creative form of music.

3. _____ Internet privacy is not good enough.

4. _____ Facebook is not good for children.

5. _____ Food should always be healthy or else the government should not allow it to be sold.

6. _____ Human vampires are real.

7. _____ Communism is a better kind of government than Capitalism.

8. _____ Pets should not be allowed in big cities.

9. _____ (Your topic here) _____

10. _____ (Your topic here) _____

 **PARTY TIME**

E Group Work/Party Time: **Stand up and speak to three members of your class and write down which topic they chose for number 1 and number 10 then write down why they chose those answers.**

Classmate **1**: (name) _____

Number 1: _____

Why? _____

Number 10: _____

Why? _____

Classmate **2**: (name) _____

Number 1: _____

Why? _____

Number 10: _____

Why? _____

Classmate **3**: (name) _____

Number 1: _____

Why? _____

Number 10: _____

Why? _____

2. CHOOSE A STRONG THESIS STATEMENT

You should make your thesis statement very strong towards your opinion. Try not to leave any doubts for someone who does not understand which side of an issue you are speaking about. State it clearly.

A. Use strong adverbs/adjectives/modals to explain your thesis statement.

[Example] The best, good, difficult, easy, should, shouldn't, must…

B. State a strong personal opinion.

[Example] Something is *immoral*, wrong, incorrect, the right way…

C. Use facts to express why your opinion is correct

[Example] The government says statistics point to, all the research shows…

F Look at the following topics and write a thesis statement that expresses a strong opinion about the topic.

1. Legalizing marijuana: _____

_____

_____

_____

2. Abortion: _____

_____

_____

_____

3. Studying more than four hours a day:

_____

_____

_____

4. Technology for young people:

_____

_____

_____

5. Online dating: _____

_____

_____

_____

3. CREATE an OUTLINE

After you have established your topic and have decided on your thesis statement you should then come up with an outline as to how you will prove your opinion. In the speech, the outline should be a simple map to help you understand how you will explain your ideas. A good outline should prepare all the basic features of your speech.

[Example outline]

Introduction

Thesis statement/Position:
People should not be allowed to have pets in big cities.

Body:
   I. The health and safety of the pet
   II. Civilization and pets
   III. Why pets are bad for people who live in big cities

Conclusion

4. VISUAL AIDS, SPEAKING NOTES and RESEARCH

After you have created your outline, research to find as much information about your topic as possible. Use the Internet and libraries in your school or city. Don't just find information that supports your opinion but look for information about what people are saying against your opinion. That information will be important.

Take notes on this information so, that you can have it readily available when you give your speech.
And make visual aids. Have pictures or art work that helps the people who are listening understand your opinion. Find visual aids that will be interesting and *shocking*. Think about how to make your presentation as interesting as possible.

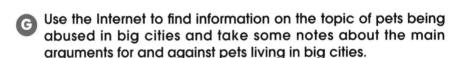

INTERNET ASSIGNMENTS [V] [W]

(G) Use the Internet to find information on the topic of pets being abused in big cities and take some notes about the main arguments for and against pets living in big cities.

PRESENTATION ACTIVITY [V] [S] [L]

Pets In The City

Would you kill a dog? Would you kick a cat that you see on the street? Do you think that pets don't have feelings? This is what you are doing if you own a pet and you live in a big city. You are slowly killing your pet if you live in a big city. It doesn't matter how rich you are or how well you **take care of** it. Having a pet in a big city like New York, London, Toronto or any other city is a slow **death sentence** to any pet. It is like **confining** that pet to a life in prison and **eventual execution**. Pets can't communicate, so we have to be aware of their physical and emotional health, and that is why it should be illegal to own a pet in any big city.

Pets should not be allowed to live in big cities because in big cities there is very little room for them to play and exercise. If there is no room, for dogs, cats, birds and all other kinds of household pets to use, then their mental and physical health are put into grave *jeopardy*. In fact the people for the Ethical Treatment of Animals (P.E.T.A) in a recent study found that most pets that live in big cities, as opposed to pets that live in the country or *rural* surroundings, have a 60% higher chance of dying sooner than other dogs. Don't kill your dog or cat. Give it the space and love that it truly deserves.

Pets are not created or designed to live in big cities. For example, dog *paws* were meant to walk and run on dirt and grass, not on concrete. Look at these images of what happens when a dog spends too much time running on concrete. They need to drink fresh water without chlorine and fluoride which most big city water treatments add to their water supply.

To have a pet in the city is to sentence your pet to a long slow death. Be a good owner and don't be *selfish*. Let pets live in a happy and healthy environment.

COMPREHENSION QUESTIONS

H Pair Work: **Listen to your partner read the speech one more time and as they are reading try to answer the following questions.**

1. What thesis statement does the speaker have?

2. Why is having a pet in a big city bad?

3. Do you think the speaker is correct in his depiction of people in big cities and pets? Why?

4. What example does the speaker give as to why dogs should not live in big cities?

5. What group does the speaker use for a statistic?

I Group Work: **Discuss the following questions in your group.**

1. Do you agree with the speaker? Why?

2. Were the visual aids effective? How so?

3. What would you have argued differently?

4. What was the most important point in the speech?

5. What could the speaker do to improve his/her next presentation?

6. Do you have arguments with the speaker's opinion? What are they?

J Make a short speech countering the arguments that the speaker made. Follow the system for creating a persuasive speech.

1. Clearly state your thesis statement.

2. Brainstorm some ideas you can use to support your thesis statement.

3. Create an outline.

4. Research, create or find some visual aids.

5. Write your speech.

 PRESENTATION ACTIVITY   S L

K Practice your speech and then vote on the best speech to present to the whole class. Present your speech to the class.

_____

_____

_____

_____

A RECIPE FOR A GREAT PERSUASIVE SPEECH

A persuasive speech requires a lot of attention to detail in the preliminary stage. There are four things you must do before you begin writing your speech so that you can create the best persuasive speech possible. The more you know before you begin writing and outlining, the easier it will be to accomplish your task effectively. Follow these four steps to help you understand your purpose and reason in order to present a good persuasive speech.

1. KNOW YOUR AUDIENCE

When you are preparing a speech you should try to know as much as you can about the people who you will give your speech to.

Making a survey:

Choose a topic that you would like to make a speech about. Write your thesis statement and then make a survey to find out how much and what, the other members of your class know about the topic.

[Example Survey]

Topic: Nuclear energy

Thesis statement:
Nuclear energy is the best and safest source of energy for the future.

Name:_____   **Country**:_____

Age:_____   **Current residence**:_____

Questions:
1. Have you ever lived in a country that used nuclear power?
2. What is your opinion of nuclear power?
3. Do you think nuclear power is safe? Why or why not?
4. What do you think is a better alternative to nuclear power? Why?
5. What do you know about nuclear power from the news?

 **L** Pair Work: **Now create your own survey.**

Topic: _____

Thesis statement: _____

Name: _____

Country: _____

Age: _____

Current residence: _____

Questions:

1. _____

2. _____

3. _____

4. _____

5. _____

 **PARTY TIME**

 M Group Work/Party time: **In groups of four or five, go around the classroom; each person asks a question. Have the group discuss the answers. Take note and tally each time your questions are answered.**

2. AUDIO VISUAL

The reason why we use visual aids is to make our message clearer and easier to understand. It is not to just repeat general information. When you think of audio visual presentations think about media that can best enhance your topic and thesis statement.

 Group Work: **From the topic you just chose for the survey, brainstorm what pictures or video would be useful to explain your topic and position. Use your cell phone or the Internet to find pictures that you can show to the class or you can draw pictures to show.**

 Group Work: **In groups show your audio visual materials and explain why it would be effective in your speech presentation.**

P Look at the following pictures and decide how they could be used in a persuasive speech, think of the topic and the position that each picture would be good for.

1. Topic: _____

Thesis statement: _____

_____

_____

2. Topic: _____

Thesis statement: _____

_____

_____

3. Topic: _____

Thesis statement: _____

_____

_____

4. Topic: _____

Thesis statement: _____

_____

_____

5. Topic: _____

Thesis statement: _____

_____

_____

6. Topic: _____

Thesis statement: _____

_____

_____

7. Topic: _____

Thesis statement: _____

_____

_____

8. Topic: _____

Thesis statement: _____

_____

_____

9. Topic: _____

Thesis statement: _____

_____

_____

10. Topic: _____

Thesis statement: _____

_____

_____

PRESENTATION ACTIVITY   S L

Q Choose one picture, a topic, and your position. Stand up in front of the class and give a speech for 45 seconds about your opinion on the topic. You only get 15 seconds to prepare.

3. TELLING A STORY

A great way to make people understand your opinion and position is to tell a short story about it.

R Pair Work: **With a partner, read the stories. Write the topic and decide what thesis statement is implied for each story.**

[Story 1]

My brother was a great athlete. He could run faster than the wind. He would always run to school, to work and everywhere he could. He would run with a big smile on his face and would inspire everyone he passed. He was chosen to represent our small town in the big city marathon. He went and came in second place. He returned to our town a hero. My brother went away to college and didn't come back for two years. At first he would call every week, but after the first year he stopped calling. When I graduated from high school, I went to visit him in college and what I saw shocked me. My brother was weak and pale. He no longer ran. In fact he seemed to be always out of breath. He couldn't hold a conversation. I noticed he hung around strange people who were always drinking and doing drugs. When I returned to my town, I didn't tell anyone, but then, three months later my brother died. He had died of an *overdose*. He would never run again. My parents were crushed. I was *distraught*.

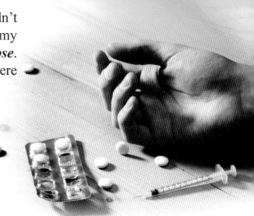

[Example]

Topic: Don't do drugs.

Thesis statement:
Thesis Statement: My brother was a great athlete but drugs ruined his life.

[Story 2]

When I was a child, I would put one penny in a piggy bank everyday. It was the best part of my adolescence. I would look forward to putting that penny in the piggy bank. When it was full my father said that he would *invest* the money for me and that if I was patient it would grow. I was very nervous but I continued to always put a penny in the piggy bank. After 20 years my father told me that all the money that I had saved and invested was now mine and that I could use it or continue saving it. I was very curious to see how much money was in the account. When I went to the bank, they showed me the account and I was surprised to find out how much my money had grown. All those pennies had grown into 1 million dollars. I was rich!

Topic: _____

Thesis statement: _____

_____

[Story 3]

I always wanted to learn English, but I was always too busy. I had an opportunity to study it in my high school, but I didn't take it seriously. It was just too *challenging* and I wasn't motivated. After high school, my friend took a year off before going to college and went to Toronto to study English at Zoni Language Centers. He had saved up some money and wanted to invest in his future. He asked me to come with him but instead I bought a *flashy* brand new car and dated all the hot girls from high school. After a year my friend came back and his English was really *fluent*. He got accepted to an *Ivy League* university in the United States while I had *splurged* all my money and *ended working* at the local laundromat. It's been five years now and I heard that my friend is the CEO of Apple computers; I wish I had been more serious about my future.

Topic: _____

Thesis statement: _____

_____

[Story 4]

Amanda was a smart girl. She was beautiful and had straight A's in school. She had a bright future in front of her. She lived in a small, rural village. She always dreamed of becoming an actress like she had seen in movies and on TV. One day, a strange man came to town and said he was a photographer for a famous magazine and was looking for models. Amanda was the first in line and because she was the most beautiful girl in the village, she was chosen to go to the big city and become a model. Amanda asked her parents but they refused, and said she could not go. That night Amanda snuck out of the house and she was never seen or heard from again. She was found dead in another country where she was sold as a victim of human trafficking.

Topic: _____

Thesis statement: _____

_____

[Story 5]

John was an ambitious person and he was always looking for a good opportunity. When his roommate asked him to help him build a website that would help people get to meet new friends from around the world, John jumped at the idea. He worked with his friend but he soon realized that his friend was not very good at it and wasn't as interested in the idea as he was. So John left and created his own company. The company is now a billion dollar web company and John is a billionaire.

Topic: _____

Thesis statement: _____

_____

⑤ Group Work: **In groups of three or four, think of a topic and thesis statement that you could write a story about to illustrate the idea you are speaking about.**

Topic: _____

Thesis statement: _____

_____

Story: _____

_____

_____

_____

_____

_____

_____

_____

T Pair Work: Look at the groups of pictures and tell a story with your partners about the pictures. Arrange the pictures in order and brainstorm what happens in between each picture. Stand up and each person present their story.

1.

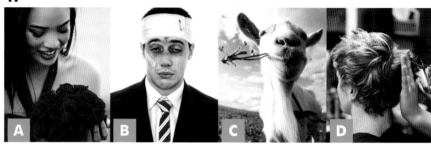

A   B   C   D

☐ → ☐ → ☐ → ☐

_____

_____

_____

2.

A   B   C   D

☐ → ☐ → ☐ → ☐

_____

_____

_____

3.

☐ → ☐ → ☐ → ☐

_____

_____

_____

4.

☐ → ☐ → ☐ → ☐

_____

_____

_____

4. A SOLUTION

You should always include in your persuasive speech a solution or reason to agree with you. A solution gives the listener a reason and opportunity to agree with your position.

[Example speech with a solution]

Topic: College students' community service

Thesis statement: All students should have to do one year of community service before graduating from college.

Story: The world needs help and volunteers to answer the call. There are many people who graduate from college and go right into the work force without ever taking a moment to see the real world and what is happening in it. No wonder that Wall Street bankers show little empathy towards middle class workers. A remedy for this situation is readily available. All students should have to do one year of community service before graduating from college.

#OCCUPYWALLST

College is supposed to teach us the value of work and the skills that we will need to be successful members of society. So, as part of college curriculum, students should be mandated to volunteer and serve those members who are less fortunate. This would provide a valuable perspective to new workers and future business leaders and politicians as well. A first hand account of the difficulties faced by the majority of working and poverty line class families would be valuable for students so that they could constantly think about how to solve some of the problems facing society as well as their own futures.

Solution: Colleges today are some of the largest institutional investors and some of the wealthiest businesses in America. Colleges should provide a year for each student to volunteer, so that they would graduate from their institutions with a strong foundation of real world experience not just classroom education. If colleges provide this service, it would make society and the world a better place.

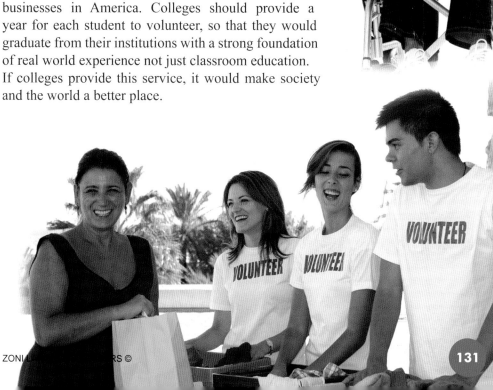

❓ COMPREHENSION QUESTIONS

U **Answer the following questions.**

1. Why does the speaker believe that this is an important topic? Do you agree?

2. How will volunteering before graduating from college help society?

3. Where would the money to pay for the year come from?

4. What paragraph has the solution to the problem of how to do the volunteering?

5. Do you agree or disagree with the speaker?

6. What are some other things the speaker could have added to make his/her argument stronger?

V Group Work: **Work in groups and think of a good solution to the following problems. Write a problem and a solution for question 5.**

1. Problem: You are standing in a crowded subway or bus and a pregnant woman gets on, but there is no empty seat and no one wants to stand up.

Solution:

_____

_____

_____

_____

2. Problem: You see someone cheating on an exam. The teacher asks you, if you saw someone cheating on the test.

Solution: _____

_____

_____

3. Problem: You go out to eat with a large group of friends and when the bill comes, you realize you don't have any money.

Solution: _____

_____

_____

4. Problem: You see a woman abusing her husband in the apartment next to you.

Solution: _____

_____

_____

5. Problem: _____

_____

Solution: _____

_____

_____

LET'S WRITE!

(W) Complete the following steps and write a short persuasive speech.

Topic: _____

_____

Thesis statement: _____

_____

Research and visual aid: _____

_____

Story: _____

_____

_____

_____

Problem: _____

_____

Solution: _____

_____

Conclusion: _____

_____

_____

See Teacher's Manual

PRESENTATION ACTIVITY

X Congratulations! You have written a persuasive speech. Now present your persuasive speech to the classroom. Prepare audio visual materials to support your speech.

HELPFUL COMMONLY-USED WORDS AND PHRASES

Common useful language for persuasive speeches: It is not enough to just blurt out your opinion or speak cold, hard facts. Persuasion is about making the listener understand and sympathize with your opinion. Below there are some expressions that you can use to help make your opinions and facts sound more down-to-earth and pleasant.

1. To clearly state your purpose:

The purpose of my talk is…
What I want you to understand from this is…
My main objective is…

2. To use the audience to agree:

As I'm sure you are well aware...
This is not new to any of you…
And any responsible person would feel the same…

3. To add emphasis:

I want to point out…
I would like to highlight the following…

4. To change the topic:

Moving on to the next topic…
OK, now let's talk about…
Turning now to …

5. To Simplify a point:

What this means is…
There are consequences to this…
The result of this is…

PRONUNCIATION DRILLS & GLOSSARY

See Teacher's Manual

Y Do Listen & Repeat (L/R) and Choral Intonation Practice of the vocabulary words and phrases in the order in which they were presented in the book. Listen to the teacher, and put the stress marks on the words.

VOCABULARY WORD	PART OF SPEECH	PRONUNCIATION	DEFINITION
cast doubt on	idiom	kast dout on	to make someone question whether something is true
catching on	phrasal Verbs	**kach**-ing on	when something becomes popular
challenging	adjective	**chal**-in-jing	very difficult
confining	adjective	kuhn-**fahyn**	feeling of being restricted and enclosed
constituents	noun	kuhn-**stich**-oo-uhnt	people of a voting community
death sentence	noun	deth **sen**-tns	the decision that someone should be put to death made by a court of law or government
distraught	adjective	dih-strawt	very disturbed of bothered
ended working	noun	endid **wur**-king	when work finishes
eventual	adjective	ih-**ven**-choo-uh	will happen at a later time or date
execution	noun	ek-si-**kyoo**-shuh	to kill someone, usually under direct orders and for a specific purpose
flashy	adjective	**flash**-ee	to wear very bright, expensive clothes and accessories
fluent	adjective	**floo**-uhnt	being able to use and understand language extremely
immoral	adjective	ih-**mawr**-uhl	directly opposite of the normal moral way of a society
intent	noun	in-**tent**	what you plan to do
invest	verb	in-**vest**	to give in order to get a financial return

Ivy League	adjective	**ahy**-vee leeg	a group of long-established north eastern U.S. colleges widely regarded as high in scholastic and social prestige
jeopardy	noun	**jep**-er-dee	the possibility of harm, death or loss, in danger
latter	noun	**lat**-er	the one after
moved by	phrasal Verb	**moovd** bahy	to arouse the emotions of, to excite and force into action
overdose	noun	**oh**-ver-dohs	take too many drugs and risk your life
paws	noun	paws	the feet of animals that have claws like a cat or dog
rural	adjective	**roor**-uhl	far away from the city; usually referring to the countryside
shocking	adjective	**shok**-ing	extreme surprise
selfish	adjective	**sel**-fish	to think only of your own interests and wants
splurged	verb	splurjd	to spend excessively without a lot of thought and just for fun
stand divided	idiom	stand dih-**vahy**-did	to be at odds and in disagreement within a group
strong foundation	idiom	strawng foun-**dey**-shuhn	a very solid and strong base for an argument or halt
take care of	phrasal verb	teyk kair ov	to provide what someone or something needs to survive
Tourette's syndrome	noun	too-**rets sin**-drohm	a disorder that has symptoms of repetitive involuntary speaking and movements
tremendous	adjective	trih-**men**-duhs	very large, prodigious
resounding	adjective	ri-**zoun**-ding	overall agreement with no doubts
rhetoric	adverb	**ret**-er-ik	effective communication primarily writing and speaking
viable	adjective	**vahy**-uh-buhl	easy to use or understand

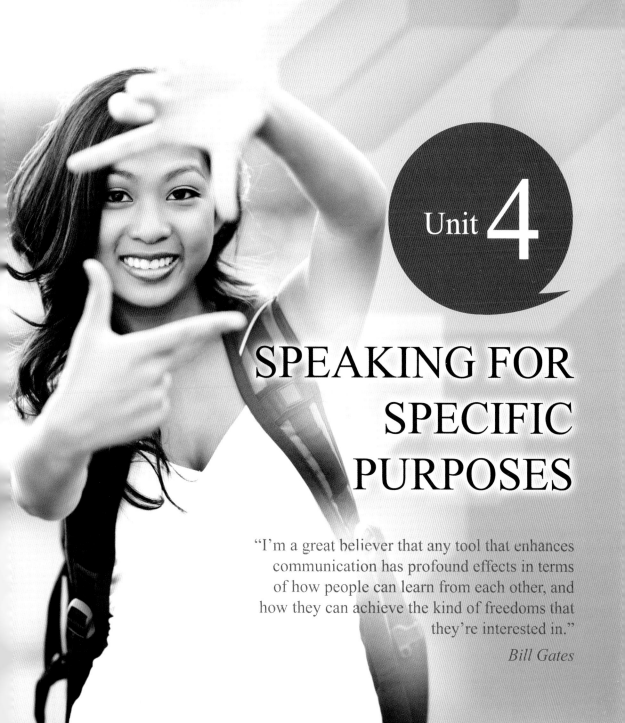

Unit 4

SPEAKING FOR SPECIFIC PURPOSES

"I'm a great believer that any tool that enhances communication has profound effects in terms of how people can learn from each other, and how they can achieve the kind of freedoms that they're interested in."

Bill Gates

WHAT IS DEBATING?

Debating is the construction of an argument for the purpose of explaining a side of a topic. We debate almost everyday of our lives. We debate every time we have to choose between two choices.

[Examples] Debating

a. Deciding what to do when hanging out with a group of friends.

b. Deciding your future.

c. Choosing the right partner.

Debating is just not battling and fighting about your opinion. Debating is following a certain structure and presentation so that you can convince others that your point of view is the most reasonable or important.

When you debate, the first thing you have to do is decide which side of the topic you want to represent, the supportive or the argumentative. All topics should have two sides to argue.

↯ PRESENTATION ACTIVITY

V S L

Example "Debating"

Why There Should Be A *Curfew* For People Under 17

Topic: A curfew for teenagers under 17.

Supportive opinion:
There should be a curfew for teenagers.
The ideal curfew would be at 11:00 p.m.

Argumentative opinion:
There should not be a curfew for teenagers.

Introduction (Supportive statement):

Hello, everyone! I would like to tell you a story about a friend of mine named Jason. He was a 9th grader in high school when we met. He was a member of the basketball team and an "A" student. One night his parents were out of town and he went to a friend's house party. The house party turned out to be a wild party that was unsupervised and *unchaperoned*, so it quickly turned into a night of *binge drinking* and drug use. All of the participants were under the age of 17 and were all in high school. Jason had too much to drink and at three in the morning decided to drive and get more beer for the party. He never made it to the store and he never made it back to the party. He had a terrible car crash while driving drunk and was *paralyzed* from the waist down. I believe that my friend Jason is paralyzed because there was a lack of supervision in his community and communities all over the world. Teenagers

everyday are *endangering* their lives and the lives of others when they stay out late without supervision and rules. To stop the tragic story of Jason from happening I believe that there should be a formal curfew for teenagers and the ideal curfew would be 11:00 p.m.

Introduction (Argumentative statement):

Teenagers must be trusted and given the opportunity to make mistakes and do the right thing. We live in a world that is very different now. Staying out late has become a normal thing for teenagers to do. There are clubs and all kinds of *legitimate* reasons why a teenager under 17 would stay out late. Curfews create criminals out of teenagers and *criminalize* the fact that they are having fun. An important part of the development process is the interaction and trust between teenagers and adults. Creating a curfew is not a good way to protect teenagers.

Rebuttal (Supportive statement):

Creating a curfew is not a sign that we do not have control of teenagers. There is, however, a responsibility that must be expected when we think about ways to protect teenagers under 17 even if it is for their own good. During the week, any reason why a teenager needs to be away from their home and family after 11 should be closely examined. The communities of the teenagers should begin to take some of the responsibility for their safety.

Rebuttal (Argumentative statement):

There have been millions of people who were 17 and went to parties after 11 and made good decisions. They didn't drink and drive. They didn't rape anyone and they didn't hurt anyone. Trust is the greatest thing we have to help inculcate to teenagers. If we trust them and believe that they will do good things then this is all that we need.

Conclusion (Supportive Statement):

Having a curfew for teenagers under 17 is not a criminalizing act. In fact, it is an act of respect and community building. Parents have the right to know where their children are and they have the right to decide the kinds of activities that their children will be involved in after 11:00 p.m. For this reason, a curfew is the only responsible way to handle many of the problems that teenagers under the age of 17 find themselves in, away from their homes at night.

Conclusion (Argumentative Statement):

A curfew for teenagers under 17 is a sign of distrust and lack of respect for the rights of teenagers. Countless generations have grown up and have learned how to cope with their social lives in a responsible way, and a curfew is a direct affront to the independence and respect teenagers deserve. An entire group should not be held accountable for accidents and a few bad apples. The best way for our teenagers to become responsible adults is to show them that we trust them and are always here for them.

 COMPREHENSION QUESTIONS

A Pair Work: **Work in pairs and answer the following questions.**

1. What happened to Jason in the introductory story? Why does the author tell this story?

2. What is the strongest argument against having a curfew for teenagers?

3. Which side of the argument do you agree with the most?

4. What is the greatest thing that we can do to help our teenagers? Do you agree?

5. What is your opinion on each side of the debate?

Aa VOCABULARY IN CONTEXT   V W

B Read the sentence using the context clues and write the meaning of the bold faced words.

1. The house party turned out to be a wild party that was unsupervised and **unchaperoned** and quickly turned into a night of **binge drinking** and drug use.

_____

_____

2. He had a terrible car crash while driving drunk and was **paralyzed** from the waist down.

_____

_____

3. Teenagers everyday are **endangering** their lives and the lives of others when they stay out late without supervision and rules.

_____

_____

4. To stop the tragic story of Jason from happening I believe that there should be a formal **curfew** for teenagers and the ideal curfew would be 11:00 p.m.

_____

_____

ZONI LANGUAGE CENTERS ©

5. There are clubs and all kinds of *legitimate* reasons for a teenager under 17 to stay out late.

_____

_____

6. Curfews make criminals out of teenagers and *criminalize* the fact that they are having fun.

_____

_____

7. It was difficult for the defense attorney to have a *rebuttal* for what the prosecution said.

_____

_____

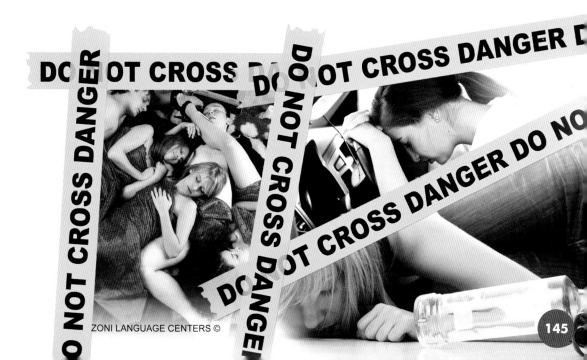

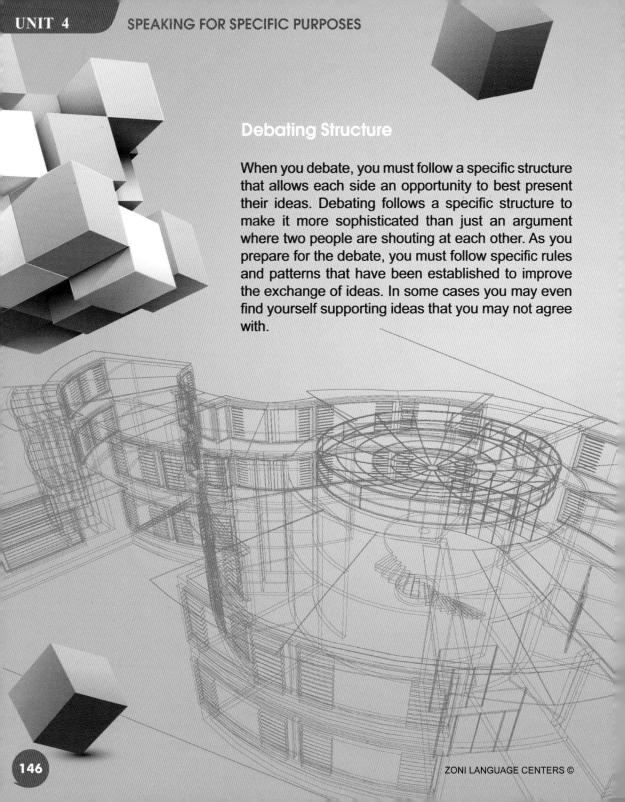

Debating Structure

When you debate, you must follow a specific structure that allows each side an opportunity to best present their ideas. Debating follows a specific structure to make it more sophisticated than just an argument where two people are shouting at each other. As you prepare for the debate, you must follow specific rules and patterns that have been established to improve the exchange of ideas. In some cases you may even find yourself supporting ideas that you may not agree with.

1. A Supportive Sentence and A Counter Argument

A supportive sentence is a sentence that helps support the opinion or perspective you are trying to debate.

A counter argument is a sentence that goes against your opinion or perspective. It could be the supporting sentence of someone who doesn't agree with your opinion.

[Example]

Topic: The world climate will change in next ten years.

Supportive sentence:

The world climate will change drastically in the next ten years because of pollution.

Counter argument:

There is no proof that climate change over the next ten years will be caused by pollution.

c Group Work: **Look at the example of a debate and try to find an example of supporting sentences and counter arguments.**

Supporting sentences:

_____

_____

Counter arguments:

_____

_____

WARM UP ACTIVITY

D Group Work: **In groups of four, look at the following questions. Then write a supportive sentence and a counter argument.**

1. Would banning guns reduce crime in the USA?

Yes: _____

_____

No: _____

_____

2. Is learning Chinese important for the global economy?

Yes: _____

No: _____

3. Should overweight people pay more to use public transportation?

Yes: _____

No: _____

4. Is space exploration important?

Yes: _____

No: _____

5. Does voting matter?

Yes: _____

No: _____

2. | Informal Debate

We debate all the time in our daily lives. When you are trying to negotiate a better business deal, you are debating. When you haggle over the price of something at a local market, you are entering into a debate. Learning formal debate procedures and techniques are important to academic life.

E Group Work: **Read the following example and answer the questions with a group.**

[Example] An informal group debating:

 John: Hey guys, I'm bored. Lets do something.

Mary: Me too.

 Carrie: What should we do?

 John: I know! Let's go to the movies and see the new Sci-Fi movie. I heard it is really good.

 Carrie: No. I don't feel like going to the movies. I would rather go to the park and have a picnic. Let's do that instead.

 John: The new Sci-Fi movie is really good, the critics say. It has five stars in all the magazines and websites. My friend from college saw it and he says it is good. Come on Carrie. We can go to the park anytime. Let's see a movie.

 Carrie: No thanks. The theater is always crowded on the weekend, and it's expensive. Also movies are never any good these days. I don't even like Sci-Fi movies. I would much rather go to the park and just hang out and have a picnic.

 John: we have both explained what we want to do. Why don't we let Mary decide?

 Carrie: Ok. Mary what should we do? **Mary**: !

1. What do John and Carrie want to do?
2. How do John and Carrie support their idea?
3. If you were Mary which one would you choose? Why?

F Group Work: **Finish the conversation for the following topics, each group must choose a different side to debate.**

1. ( ): I think there are too many requirements to get a visa to come to the United States. It is a slow and time-consuming process.

( ): It is important to have a lot of rules and regulations so you can be sure that people who are coming to the United States have good intentions.

( ): _____

_____

_____

( ): _____

_____

_____

2. ( ): Recycling is very important and all people should be required to recycle, no matter what country they live in.

( ): Recycling is important but it should be voluntary because it takes a lot of time and energy.

( ): _____

_____

_____

( ): _____

_____

_____

3. (   ): The economy in my country is going to improve and everything will be ok.

(   ): The economy of my country is only going to get worse, so it is important to prepare for its collapse.

(   ): _____

_____

_____

(   ): _____

_____

_____

4. (   ): Fashion is important.

(   ): Fashion is ridiculous, and there is no point to it.

(   ): _____

_____

_____

(   ): _____

_____

_____

NOTE

In all of these examples (**1-5**) you have different sides that you can choose from and you should make a choice based upon the information you have available.

5. (   ): Same sex marriage is an important right that should be allowed in every country.

(   ): I don't think same sex marriage will ever be accepted in my country.

(   ): _____

_____

_____

(   ): _____

_____

_____

G Look at the following pictures and decide which you would choose and explain why.

1. Which food would you like to eat?

Why? _____

_____

_____

_____

2. Which would you like as a pet?

Why? _____

_____

_____

_____

Morgan Freeman   *Madonna*

3. Who would you rather be?

Why? _____

_____

_____

_____

4. Where would you like to go on vacation?

Why? _____

_____

_____

_____

Group Work

H Group Work: **Explain your choice and continue the informal debating with a group.**

NOTE

Research is an important part of debating. You must be prepared to support your side of the topic but also to rebut the main points that the opposition will introduce.

① Pair Work: **Work with a partner, choose one from the following supportive sentences 1-5, make a counter argument and then make a supportive and argumentative statement.**

1. The world should set a drinking age at 31.
2. Fashion should be taught in all high schools.
3. Marijuana should be legalized.
4. Prostitution should be legalized.
5. Women are superior to men in business.

Counter argument:

_____

Supportive statement:

_____

_____

_____

_____

Argumentative statement:

_____

_____

_____

_____

3. Formal debate

A formal debating should follow a basic structure. The introductory argument is the first time you speak and argue for your point. After that, the other side will get an opportunity to present their ideas. Next, you will get a chance to rebut ideas that the other person presented. Then, there will be a conclusion after all arguments and rebuttals have been made.

 J Group Work: **Read the example and complete the following steps.**

[Example] Formal debating:

Topic:

Should corporations and extremely rich people pay more taxes than poor people?

Group 1 (Supportive sentence):

Yes, corporations and extremely rich people should pay more taxes than poor people.

Group 2 (Counter argument):

No, corporations and extremely rich people should not pay more taxes than poor people.

ZONI LANGUAGE CENTERS ©

Step 1 **Write two more reasons to support your opinion.**

Group 1: Introduction (Supportive statement)

Reason **1**: Rich people should pay more taxes because historically when there is a large amount of growth in an economy; it is because of the taxes from corporations and its wealthiest individuals.

Reason **2**: _____

_____

_____

Reason **3**: _____

_____

_____

Group 2: Introduction (Argumentative statement)

Reason **1**: Corporations and the wealthiest Americans should not be taxed more because it is not fair to tax someone more just because they are more successful than others.

Reason **2**: _____

_____

_____

Reason **3**: _____

_____

_____

Step 2 **Write one more rebuttal statement.**

Group 1: Rebuttal (Supportive statement)

Rebuttal statement **1**: Corporations and the extremely wealthy have made their money because of the freedoms and laws of the country that support them, so it would be fair to charge them more taxes.

Rebuttal statement **2**: _____

_____

_____

_____

Group 2: Rebuttal (Argumentative statement)

Rebuttal statement **1**: Taxing corporations and the extremely wealthy is not the only reason that economies flourish. There are many factors that contribute to economic growth and taxes are just a small part of it.

Rebuttal statement **2**: _____

_____

_____

_____

ZONI LANGUAGE CENTERS ©

Step 3 Write the conclusion.

Group 1: Conclusion (Supportive statement)

_____

_____

_____

_____

_____

Group 2: Conclusion (Argumentative statement)

_____

_____

_____

_____

_____

See Teacher's Manual

Congratulations!
You have just made a formal debate!

LET'S DEBATE!   W S

K Make a list of three topics that you would find interesting to debate.

1. _____

2. _____

3. _____

PRESENTATION ACTIVITY   W S L

L Group Work: In groups, discuss all of the topics that you came up with and decide on one topic to debate. Each person should fill out the rest of the information according to their side of the debate.

[Debating Outline]

1. Supportive sentence: _____

_____

2. Three supportive statements to support your side:

   a. _____

_____

_____

b. _____

_____

_____

c. _____

_____

_____

3. The best rebuttal statement against your side.

_____

_____

_____

_____

4. Conclusion:

_____

_____

_____

_____

_____

_____

WARM UP ACTIVITY

M Group Work: In groups, look at the pictures and choose three pictures and explain how you think they are related to each other. Be creative, don't look for the obvious. Share your answers with the other members of your group.

Nicki Minaj

E

F

G

H

Daniel Craig

Three pictures: ☐ ☐ ☐

_____

_____

_____

_____

_____

_____

🔍 WHAT IS AN IMPROMPTU SPEECH?

An impromptu speech is a speech given with little or no time to prepare. There are many reasons why you would need to give an impromptu speech.

1. You have been asked to fill in for someone else at the last minute.
2. You were asked to be on a panel or give a group presentation.
3. You are answering questions from a group or individuals at your work.
4. You are being interviewed for a job or on the radio.
5. You are part of a debate.
6. You are asked to make a speech at a party.

While you may never know on what occasion you may have to give an impromptu speech, you can always be prepared by understanding the basics and foundation of good speech writing, so that you can just plug in the information.

For a good impromptu speech remember to follow the same procedures you would for any speech.

1. Create an interesting Introduction.
   a. Tell a story
   b. Give a quote

PRESENTATION ACTIVITY

See Teacher's Manual

Example "Impromptu Speeches"

[Example 1]

Situation: It was meant to be, *or so it seems*. The Boston Wildcats basketball team is losing. It is halftime, and everyone has *low morale*. This is the final game of the season and it looks like the basketball team will lose. Thomas, a small *third string* player who nobody even remembers, suddenly stands up, and with determination in his eyes and a *booming voice* begins an impromptu speech hoping to motivate the team to a victory.

Thomas's impromptu speech:

Introduction: I *have had enough*! I look out and into the stadium and I see disappointed friends and family members who came to see us win. But instead they see a team that is arguing, *timid* and afraid. Why are we afraid?

Important point: We have earned the right to compete here tonight. It doesn't matter that we are *the underdogs*. It is all right to be imperfect, But let's not run away from our destiny. We have a chance to create our own destiny. To be the leaders of our own futures, let's not give up this chance. We have the opportunity to shock the world, and we can't pass up this chance. We will not go silently into the night! We will fight! We will fight! We will fight!

Consequence: Everyone jumps up and starts chanting; We will fight! We will fight! The team went back out onto the court and won the game.

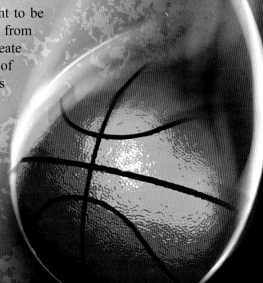

[Example 2]

Situation: Jeff's best friend Brad is getting married. Jeff is the best man and he must *give a toast* at the reception dinner after the wedding. He has written down exactly what he wants to say. However he lost his speech, and he just realized it a few minutes before he has to give the speech. Everyone turns to look at him as the bride and groom ask him to give the traditional and honorary toast.

Jeff's impromptu speech:

Introduction: Thank you, everyone. I am so happy to be here. I have known, the groom Brad, for over twenty years. And the bride Sandy for about six.

Important point: And the one thing I can tell you for sure is that they were *made for each other*. They *fit together like a hand in a glove*, and *two peas in a pod*. I used to think that true love didn't exist, but because of this union today I am a born again believer in true love because I see it right here in front of me. I see the way that these two *love birds* communicate and help each other grow, mentally, spiritually and emotionally. I only hope one day I will be as lucky as the two of you. To the bride and groom. May you be happy forever.

Consequence: Everyone raises their drink and cheers the bride and groom wishing them luck and happiness in their married life.

N After you have completed your introduction, the next step is to come up with the important points that you want to talk about in your impromptu speech. Look at the following example situations and answer each question.

1. You have been asked to give a toast at the reception dinner of your best friend's wedding. What are three important points that you would like to talk about?

a. _____

b. _____

c. _____

2. You are at a job interview for <u>(job)</u> _____ and the interviewer asks why you should get the job. What are three important points you could say?

a. _____

b. _____

c. _____

3. You are an ambassador from your country to another country and a reporter asks you to describe the good things about your country. What are three important points you could say?

a. _____

b. _____

c. _____

PRACTICE ACTIVITY

Group Work: Think about a story for each of the topics listed below. In groups, write a story. Further, discuss how you can write an impromptu speech. Start from an introduction, and then make important points.

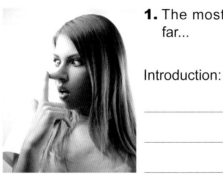

1. The most important lesson of my life so far...

Introduction: _____

_____

_____

_____

Important points: _____

_____

_____

_____

_____

2. Laughter is the best medicine.

Introduction: _____

_____

_____

_____

_____

Important points: _____

_____

_____

_____

_____

3. Beauty is always in the eye of the beholder.

Introduction: _____

_____

_____

_____

_____

Important points: _____

_____

_____

_____

_____

4. If I were an animal I'd be a (n)...

Introduction: _____

_____

_____

_____

_____

Important points: _____

_____

_____

_____

_____

5. Real love is not the stuff of pop songs.

Introduction: _____

_____

_____

_____

_____

Important points: _____

_____

_____

_____

_____

INTERNET ASSIGNMENTS

W S L

P Using Google, look up a quote that expresses your opinion about the following topics. In groups of four, let each person choose one quote and explain its meaning.

1. War

Quote: _____

_____

2. Relationships

Quote: _____

_____

3. Travel

Quote: _____

_____

4. Education

Quote: _____

_____

5. Family

Quote: _____

_____

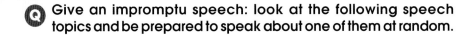

PRESENTATION ACTIVITY

Q Give an impromptu speech: look at the following speech topics and be prepared to speak about one of them at random.

1. The world is a smaller place these days.

2. If I ruled the world...

3. Team sports build strong individuals.

4. Who has been the most influential person in your life and why?

5. How we look is unimportant. It's who we are on the inside that counts.

6. Summer is the best and worst of times. Why?

7. Real learning doesn't occur in a classroom.

8. What is normal is decided by the society we live in.

9. Art is essential to life.

10. A sense of humor is essential.

HELPFUL COMMONLY-USED WORDS AND PHRASES

Sometimes the best way to persuade is by using an idiom to give the exact meaning of the information or feeling you are trying to convey. An idiom can go right to the heart of the listener and provide a deeper meaning and understanding to your reasons and opinions. Many times we find ourselves trying to persuade others about our opinion by using complex and technical language. The interjection of an idiom to exactly express the point you want to make is a very savvy way to add character to your persuasive speeches. Take a look at the following idioms and see how you could use them in your next speech, debate or presentation.

 1. *Like talking to a brick wall*: said of trying unsuccessfully to persuade or reason with someone.

[Example] I hate talking to Republicans about global warming because when it comes to the facts it is like talking to a brick wall.

 2. *Talk in circles*: to speak in a confusing or indirect manner

[Example] The lawyer was unprepared and the judge accused him of talking in circles to hide that fact from the jury.

 3. *Hook, line, and sinker*: to completely believe and trust something.

[Example] He fell for the idea hook, line, and sinker.

 4. *How do you like them, apples?*: This idiomatic expression is used to express surprise or shock at something that has happened. It can also be used to boast about something you have done.

[Example] I won! I won! I won the lottery. How do you like them, apples? I'm rich.

PRONUNCIATION DRILLS & GLOSSARY

R Do Listen & Repeat (L/R) and Choral Intonation Practice of the vocabulary words and phrases in the order in which they were presented in the book. Listen to the teacher, and put the stress marks on the words.

VOCABULARY WORD	PART OF SPEECH	PRONUNCIATION	DEFINITION
binge drinking	noun	binj driŋk	getting drunk by drinking a lot of alcohol or drinking many days in a row
booming voice	noun	boom-ing vois	very loud and deep voice
criminalize	adjective	**krim**-uh-nl-ahyz	to make someone or something appear to be criminal or illegal
curfew	noun	**kur**-fyoo	a specific time that you must be home
endanger	verb	en-**deyn**-jeyr	to put in harm's way
fit together like a hand in a glove	idiom	fit tuh-geth-er lahyk ey hand in ey gluhv	when something seems natural and normal together
give a toast	Idiom	giv ey tohst	to give an informal speech on a special occasion.
have had enough	phrasal verbs	hav had ih-nuhf	to be completely finished and done with a situation not to your liking
legitimate	adjective	li-**jit**-uh-meyt	legal and correct
love birds	idiom	luhv burds	two people who are affectionate and in love

low morale	noun	loh muh-**ral**	feeling unmotivated, bored, and or depressed
made for each other	idiom	meyd fawr eech uhth-er	the feeling that two people have so much in common that they are soul mates
or so it seems	phrase	awr soh it seems	what guessing, and clues lead you to believe
paralyzed	adjective	**par**-uh-lahyzd	being unable to move
rebuttal	noun	ri-**buht**-l	a response to an opinion you do not agree with
the underdogs	idiom	th ee **uhn**-der-dawgs	the person who is most likely to lose in a confrontation or competition
third string	idiom	thurd string	last possible substitute for sports athletes
timid	adjective	**tim**-id	shy, bashful, introverted
two peas in a pod	idiom	too pees in ey pod	very close friends
unchaperoned	adjective	uhn **shap**-uh-rohn	not watched; with no adult guidance

Unit 5

WRITE, EDIT and PRESENT

"There are always three speeches, for every one you actually gave. The one you practiced, the one you gave, and the one you wish you gave."

Dale Carnegie

1 INFORMATIVE SPEECH

What Is Love?

 **WARM UP ACTIVITY**

A Pair Work: **Discuss the following questions with your partner.**

1. Have you ever been in love?
2. What are certain behaviors typical of people in love?
3. What feeling is similar to love?
4. Why do you think love is important?
5. Where does love come from?
6. What is a biological clock?
7. Can someone think he/she is in love but not really be in love? Give an example.

ASSESSMENT EXERCISE: PROCESS OF THE SPEECH

See Teacher's Manual

B Read the final presentation on page 181, and complete the following outline.

[OUTLINE]

☑ Introduction:
Thesis statement:
Love doesn't come from our hearts;
it comes from our brains.

☑ Body: Topic sentence (Main idea):
The chemical dopamine is released into
the brain to create the feeling of love.

☐ Example anecdote:

☐ Conclusion:

a. **DOPAMINE**

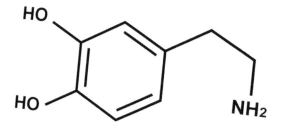

ubstantia nigra,
opamine -
roducing cells

b.

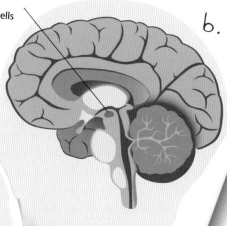

c.

d.

Play list
Can You Feel the Love
My Heart Will Go On
From The Bottom Of...
I Got You Babe
Crazy In Love

☑ Audio visual

1. Illustration diagram
    a: The chemical formula of Dopamine
    b: Cross-sectional view of the brain:
        showing where dopamine comes from
2. Pictures:
    c: A woman making a heart shape with
        her hands
    d: A woman holding a puppy
3. BGM: From The Bottom Of My Heart
    (Stevie Wonder)

☑ Final Presentation

What Is Love?

When we think of love, we think about the *bubbly* feeling of emotions that *emanate* somewhere from our heart. But the truth is a lot less romantic idea. Love doesn't come from our hearts. In fact, while we have looked at Cupid *starry-eyed* and in *bewilderment*, science has found out that love is no more than a brain process and chemical reaction. To put it *bluntly*, love is the brain's reaction to stimulus by releasing the chemical dopamine into the brain.

Dopamine is a chemical *neurotransmitter* that causes the body to feel good and have positive feelings. Love doesn't come from our hearts; it comes from our brains. Let's explore two examples of how love is created. Amanda is a beautiful girl. As she walks down the street everyday to go to work she passes the house of her neighbor Tom. Every time Tom sees Amanda, dopamine is released in his brain. This chemical process of releasing neurotransmitters into his brain every

time Amanda walks by creates a feeling of *euphoria* and happiness for Tom. His brain is now becoming used to the feeling of euphoria every time Amanda walks by. Amanda, however, doesn't notice Tom. So, her brain continues to function normally and doesn't release any dopamine. Until Tom finds a puppy one day, and he is giving it a bath outside as Amanda walks by. Amanda sees the puppy and her brain releases dopamine at the sight of the puppy. She walks over and tells Tom how cute the puppy is and Tom's brain releases more dopamine. This is a very simplistic example of how love is just a chemical reaction in our brain. The truth is, there are many determining factors that would lead to the release of dopamine. But, in our example, Tom believes he is in love with Amanda and Amanda has fallen in love with the puppy. The release of dopamine in the brain has created the effect of being in love.

In conclusion, love is a feeling and emotion that we have always assumed to be generated in the heart, but what science has proven to us is that love is actually just a simple chemical reaction in the brain. How romantic is that?

LET'S WRITE!

C Complete the following steps and write an informative speech.

[OUTLINE]

☐ Topic:

☐ Title:

☐ Reason why you are choosing this speech:

☐ Introduction (Hook/Attention getters): How will you introduce your speech?

☐ Thesis statement:

☐ Body:
Topic sentence (main idea) 1:

Topic sentence (main idea) 2:

Topic sentence (main idea) 3:

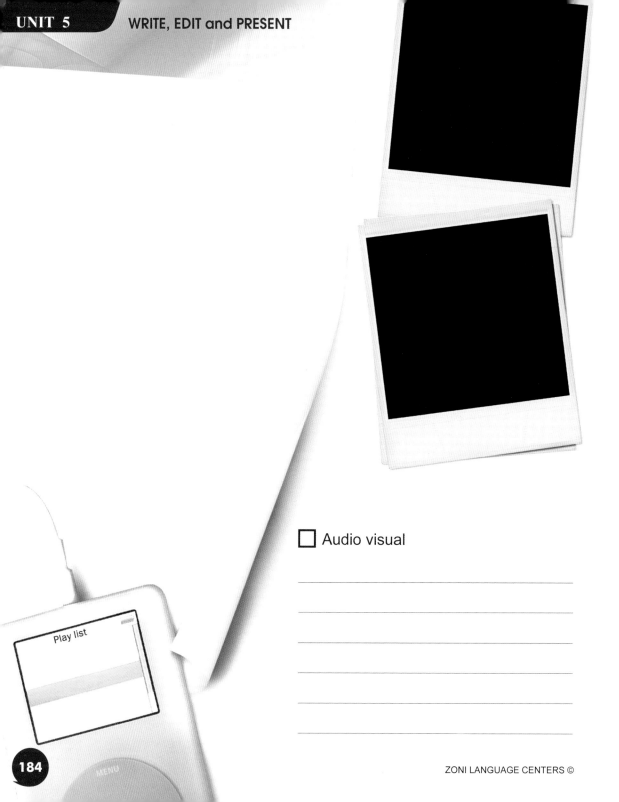

☐ Audio visual

_____

_____

_____

_____

_____

_____

Play list

☐ Final presentation

_____

_____

_____

_____

_____

_____

_____

_____

_____

PRESENTATION ACTIVITY

D Pair Work: Practice your speech with your partner and present it to the class.

2 DEBATING

Mixed Martial Arts (MMA)

 **WARM UP ACTIVITY**

E Pair Work: **Discuss the following questions with your partner.**

1. Have you heard of the UFC? What was your first impression?
2. Do they have Mixed Martial Arts tournaments in your country?
3. Which sport do you think is safer; Ice Skating, Boxing or MMA?
4. Have you ever been trained in martial arts? Which one? Why?
5. Have you ever had to defend yourself in a fight?
6. Which fighting style is famous in your country?

ASSESSMENT EXERCISE: PROCESS OF THE SPEECH

See Teacher's Manual

F Read the introduction (supportive statement) on page 189, and complete the following outline to make the debate.

[OUTLINE]

☑ Topic:
What is Mixed Martial Arts (MMA).

☑ Supportive opinion:
Mixed Martial Arts is the best fighting style to learn.

☐ Argumentative opinion:

a.

b.

c.

d.

☑ Audio visual

1. DVD: Anderson Silva " Like Water2. "

2. a: Pictures: mixed fighting (championship,
        2009, Russia),

   b: Judo (World CUP, Romania, 2011),

   c: Kung-Fu (Martial Arts Show, China),

   d: Boxing (World's Unrivalled Fight, 2011,
        Thailand)

3. BGM: Hero: Overture, Crouching Tiger
        Hidden Dragon, Street Fighting

Play list
Crouching Tiger, ...
Kempo and Kumite
Hero: Overture
Matin d'orient
Street Fighting

☑ Introduction (Supportive statement)

Mixed Martial Arts (MMA)

MMA is the best fighting style to learn. MMA brings together many styles of fighting. It *incorporates* the best parts of various fighting *disciplines* such as Kung-fu, Brazilian Jiu-jitsu and Boxing. In the early 1900's, a sport called anything goes fighting, which was called Vale Tudo in Brazil, sparked interest in the idea that had been around since the beginning of time. Which fighting style was the best? In Denver in 1993, a tournament was created to match up many different fighting styles with the hope of finding out which one was the best. The tournament was called the Ultimate Fighting Championship and it was a *smashing* success. The first winner of this event was a Brazilian Jiu-Jitsu fighter named Royce Gracie and even though he was smaller than his opponent, he was able to beat his opponent by using *grappling* and lock techniques to subdue him. However, the sport soon turned very violent and bloody and was banned from cable TV. To this day, it is still illegal in a few states including New York. From these early matches fighters began to realize that they had to train many different ways of fighting in order to *spar* with each other, and so MMA was born. MMA trains many different disciplines and fighting styles so that you are always prepared for anything.

LET'S WRITE!

See Teacher's Manual

G **Pair Work: Expand** on the topic (MMA) for debate and choose another form of martial arts as a topic for counter debate. Complete the following steps and write a debating presentation. Use the appropriate tools and format for a debate presentation.

Examples of the fight styles:

• Kung-fu	• Boxing	• Wrestling	• Kickboxing	• Karate
• Brazilian Jiu-jitsu	• Muay Thai	• Capoeira	• Aikido	• Ninjutsu
• Jeet Kune Do	• Arnis	• Tae Kwon Do		

[OUTLINE]

☐ Topic:

☑ Supportive opinion:

Mixed Martial Arts is the best fighting style to learn.

Presenter name: _____

☐ Argumentative opinion:

Presenter name: _____

☐ Introduction (Supportive statement):

☐ Introduction (Argumentative statement):

☐ Rebuttal (Supportive statement):

☐ Rebuttal (Argumentative statement):

☐ Conclusion (Supportive statement):

☐ Conclusion (Argumentative statement):

☐ Audio visual

See Teacher's Manual

☐ Final presentation

_____

_____

_____

_____

_____

_____

_____

_____

Pair Practice

 PRESENTATION ACTIVITY S L

H Pair Work: **Practice your debate with your group and present it to the class.**

See Teacher's Manual

3 PERSUASIVE SPEECH

Gun Ban

Pair Practice

WARM UP ACTIVITY

S L

1 Pair Work: **Discuss the following questions with your partner.**

1. Do you or any of your friends and relatives possess a gun?

2. What do you think is the purpose of having a gun?

3. Is it easy to have a gun in your country? What are the procedures and requirements to be able to purchase a gun?

4. Should all people carry a gun? Why or why not?

5. What other weapons are good for security and protection, other than a gun.?

6. Should all people have a gun? Why or why not?

ASSESSMENT EXERCISE: PROCESS OF THE SPEECH   W

J Read the final presentation "Gun Ban" on page 197, and find the Introduction, thesis statement, main idea (body), supporting sentences and conclusion.

[OUTLINE]

☐ Thesis statement:

☐ Introduction: attention getter:

☐ Body: Supporting sentences:

☐ Body:
Topic sentences (Main ideas):

☐ Conclusion:

c.

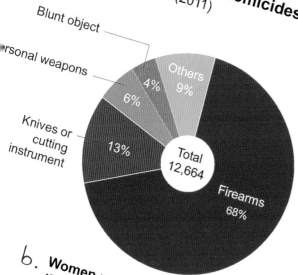

a. **Weapon of Choice in Homicides**
USA (2011)

Blunt object

Personal weapons

Others
9%

4%

6%

Knives or
cutting
instrument

13%

Total
12,664

Firearms
68%

d.

b. **Women murdered by
their intimate partners**
USA (2010)

Homicides per million
female residents

States that
do not require
a background
check for
private
handgun sales

-38%

States that
require
a background
check for
private
handgun sales

5.09

3.17

☑ Audio visual

1. Chart:

  a: Weapon of Choice in Homicide/USA (2011)

  b. Women murdered by their intimate
     partners (Comparison of states that
     do not require background check for
     private handgun sales with states that
     do require)

2. Pictures:

  c: Charlton Heston

  d: AK-47

PRESENTATION ACTIVITY

☑ Final presentation

Gun Ban

"From my cold, dead hands." These were the words once used by Charlton Heston, Hollywood actor and President of the National Rifle Association (NRA) from 1998-2003, at an NRA rally to summarize his opinion on the topic of gun control. It was his way of warning the U.S. government that any attempt to *restrict* his right to *bear arms* would be met with the *fiercest* of resistance, *fundamentalism* making abundantly clean. The reaction of those in attendance was thundering, *rapturous* applause.

After all, the right to bear arms is the Second Amendment to the American Constitution, behind only to the right to assembly and press, religion, and the Bill of Rights is *inviolable*. Firearms have been a part not just of the American culture, but of human history, for hundreds of years. It was with firearms that the War of Independence was won, and the American "Wild West" tamed. Nearly every Hollywood blockbuster

features gunfights and shoot-outs as a part of the spectacle. Their iconic heroes look cool as they proudly wield their deadly weapons.

However, in the wake of a series of public massacres by ordinary American citizens, there has been increasing public demand to put *harsher* restrictions on who can buy guns, how many and what type can they buy. Such measures, contrary to what their opponents might argue, would not be a violation of the Second Amendment, and they would reduce the violent crime rate. It is therefore important to introduce these new gun laws and ensure their strict enforcement.

"From our cold, dead hands!" come the shouts from the pro-gun lobby. "You'd be violating our constitutional rights!" The fear is not only that the government would take away everyone's guns, but also that such action would set a dangerous precedent that could lead to the *stripping away* of other basic freedoms as protected by the Bill of Rights. But look at the wording of the second amendment, and it becomes very clear that the Founding Fathers intended the right to bear arms only for use in the context of a state-organized militia, not some every-man-for-himself Darwinian society leaving all individuals to their own devices for protection and survival. (In recent years, the Supreme Court has ruled that the Second Amendment does extend beyond a state-run militia and can apply to individual citizens bearing arms as well.) In any event, the issue is not whether to issue an *all-encompassing* ban on every privately owned firearm in the country, but rather to make big-picture decisions on gun control such as outlawing assault weapons, those guns most *notorious* for violence and murder in American society. After all, is a military-standard AK-47 really necessary to protect one's home?

Some may argue that yes, such heavy firepower is necessary as this is what criminals and gangs use, and banning these weapons will only prevent law-abiding citizens from having access to them. But does this argument stand up? Are we really safer with such a *proliferation* of guns available to every man, woman and child in the country (nearly three-hundred million, a 1:1 ratio of guns to citizens)? There were 11,101 gun-related *homicides* in the U.S. in 2011. Two-thirds of all homicides in the U.S. involve a firearm of some sort. It has been found that fatalities are 300% more likely to occur during robberies where guns are involved. The same is true in instances of domestic violence turning deadly, nearly triple when guns are involved. There is one firearm-related death in the U.S. for every ten-thousand citizens every year. Compare these numbers with Great Britain, a nation of sixty-two million people, where there are approximately seven guns for every one hundred citizens. In 2011, there were only 38 gun related homicides. That's right, 38! The ***correspondence*** between the proliferation of guns and gun-related deaths couldn't be clearer, and it is high time the U.S. government did something about it.

The good news is that gun ownership in the U.S. is on the decline, from 50% in 1973 to around 30% today. The Obama administration proposed new laws in 2013 that would ***curtail*** gun violence, including stricter background checks, education funding, a ban on assault weapons and a limit on the number of bullets someone can buy. Of course, even such common-sense measures are being stubbornly opposed by the NRA and other pro-gun lobbies, who cry out from behind the facade of the second amendment about civil rights being ***violated*** and the incredible doublethink argument that more guns mean less violence. The firearm industry is a multi-million dollar business, and these lobbyists are simply protecting their business. It's just a shame that this particular business results in thousands of cold, dead hands every year.

By Charles Heil, Principal South Chelsea College, London

WRITE, EDIT and PRESENT

PRONUNCIATION DRILLS & GLOSSARY V S L

See Teacher's Manual

K Do Listen & Repeat (L/R) and Choral Intonation Practice of the vocabulary words and phrases in the order in which they were presented in the book. Listen to the teacher, and put the stress marks on the words.

VOCABULARY WORD	PART OF SPEECH	PRONUNCIATION	DEFINITION
all-encompassing	adjective	**awl**-en-**kuhm**-puh-sing	to include everything
bear arms	phrasal Verb	bair ahrm	to have guns prepared for use
bewilderment	noun	bih-wil-der-muh nt	when you are confused
bluntly	adverb	bluhnt ly	to express without care or worry
bubbly	adjective	**buhb**-lee	very happy feeling
correspondence	noun	kawr-uh-**spon**-duh ns	to be in communication with someone using letters
curtail	verb	ker-**teyl**	to stop from happening
disciplines	noun	dis-uh-plin s	different styles united by one common experience
emanate	verb	**em**-uh-neyt	the process of coming from an original source
euphoria	noun	yoo-**fawr**-ik, -**for**-	a feeling of extreme happiness
fiercest	adjective	feers **est**	the superlative form of fierce meaning the absolute highest level of anger

ZONI LANGUAGE CENTERS ©

fundamentalism	noun	fuhn-duh-**men**-tl-iz-uh m	to strictly follow something with absolute faith and conviction
grappling	noun	**grap**-ling	a close, hand-to-hand fight
harsher	adjective	hahrsh er	comparative form of harsh meaning more abrasive, difficult or unpleasant
homicide	noun	**hom**-uh-sahyd	murder
incorporate	verb	in-**kawr**-puh-reyt	to combine and form into one thing
inviolable	adjective	in-**vahy**-uh-luh-buh l	impossible to change or destroy
neurotransmitter	noun	noo r-oh-**trans**-mit-er	chemicals in your brain that send information
notorious	adjective	noh-**tawr**-ee-uh s	to have a bad reputation; infamous
proliferation	noun	pruh-lif-uh-**rey**-shuh n	to spread quickly
rapturous	adjective	**rap**-cher-uh s	extreme peace and happiness
restrict	verb	ri-**strikt**	to place rules and regulations to on specific freedoms
smashing	adjective	**smash**-ing	to destroy into little pieces, or destroy by flattening
spar	verb	spahr	fighting for training purposes
starry-eyed	adjective	**stahr**-ee-ahyd	hope/ dream about something
stripping away	verb	strip ing uh-**wey**	to take something from something else by force
violated	adjective	**vahy**-uh-leyt ed	to disrespect, do what you are not supposed to do

Final Oral Exam

See Teacher's Manual

Prepare a persuasive speech for your final oral exam, and come up with a detailed outline of your presentation. Please draw and write a brief description of the audio visual materials that you will be using corresponding your outline.

Take notes from your Internet research.

[OUTLINE]

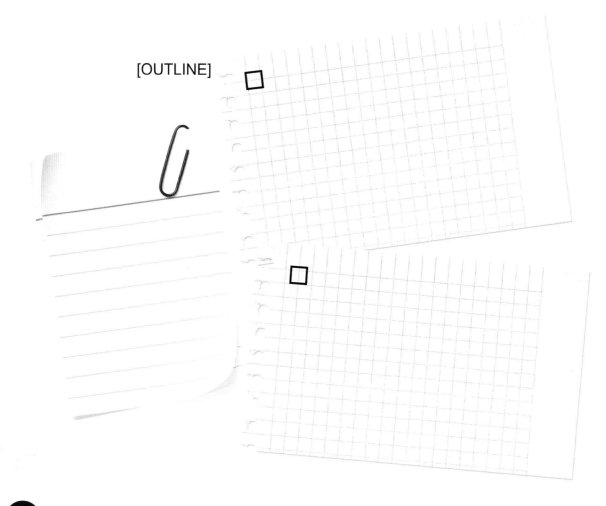

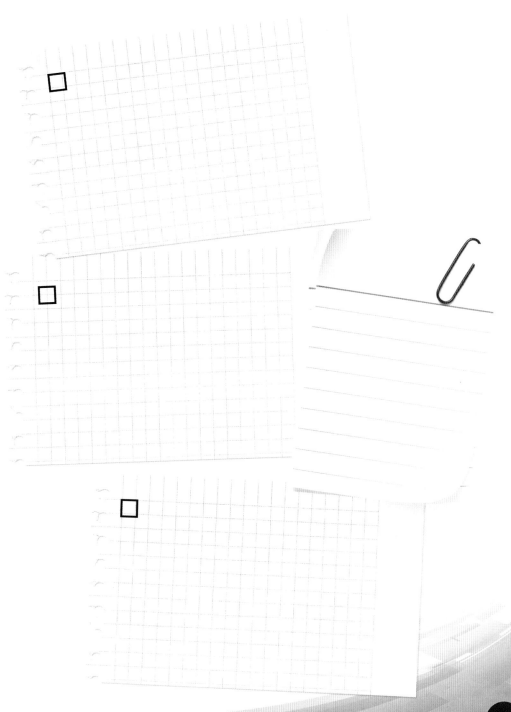

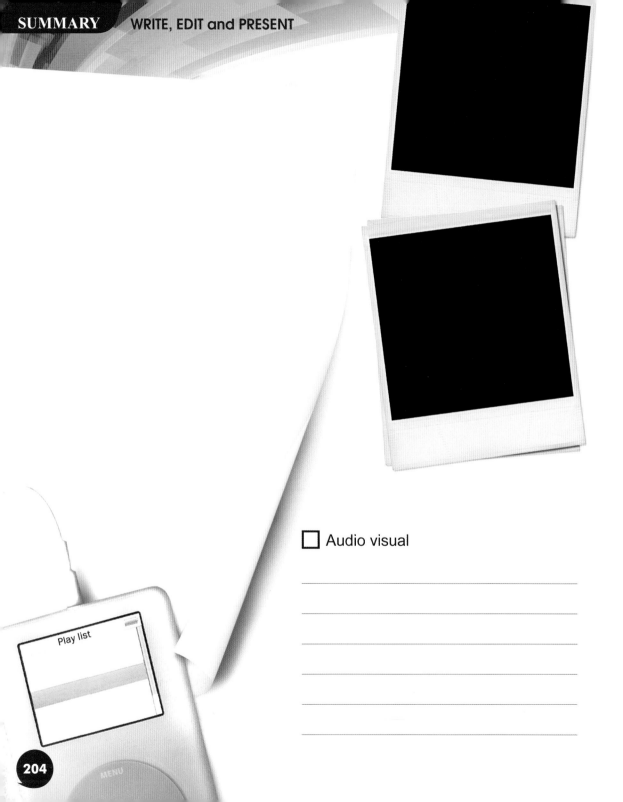

☐ Audio visual

☐ Final presentation

_____

_____

_____

_____

_____

_____

_____

_____

_____

🎤 FINAL ORAL EXAM PRESENTATION   S L

Deliver your speech following all the techniques in speech delivery. Please use the form as a guide on how your speech is going to be graded.

And remember, have a great time!

Congratulations!

You have finished Zoni English System 11

Speech Diagnostic

Purpose: Students will prepare a self introductory speech for 3-4 minutes and be rated accordingly. Since this is their first speech, there will be an audio/video recording of the entire presentation. This will be used as a diagnostic test to identify student's skills in delivering speeches/presentation prior to taking this course. This will serve as a a indicator of how students have improved their presentation skills both in content and form as they progress throughout the course.

Name of Student: _____

Date: _____ / _____ / _____

Final Grade

Content	Rating					Comments
1. Introduction (Background)	1	2	3	4	5	
2. Information about family	1	2	3	4	5	
3. Current situation	1	2	3	4	5	
4. Hobbies/Interests	1	2	3	4	5	
5. Future plans	1	2	3	4	5	
6. Other supporting details	1	2	3	4	5	
7. Organization/unity of ideas	1	2	3	4	5	
8. Use of visual aids	1	2	3	4	5	

Content Grade

Form	Rating					Comments
1. Posture/Gestures	1	2	3	4	5	
2. Facial expressions	1	2	3	4	5	
3. Tone/Volume of voice	1	2	3	4	5	
4. Enthusiasm	1	2	3	4	5	
5. Time limit	1	2	3	4	5	

Form Grade

Rating Key: 1 = Poor   2 = Fair   3= Good   4= Very Good   5= Excellent

Additional Comments/Suggestions: _____

_____

_____

_____

Informative Speech

Purpose: This form is used to evaluate how students can state their ideas simply, clearly and interestingly. This is also a test on how knowledgeable they are about their chosen topic and how effectively they delivered the information.

┌─ Final Grade ─┐

Name of Student: _____

Date: _____ / _____ / _____

Content	Rating	Comments
1. Attention getting opener	1 2 3 4 5	
2. Preview	1 2 3 4 5	
3. Organization	1 2 3 4 5	
4. Supporting materials	1 2 3 4 5	
5. Visual aids	1 2 3 4 5	
6. Transitions	1 2 3 4 5	
7. Summary	1 2 3 4 5	
8. Concluding remarks	1 2 3 4 5	

Content Grade

Form	Rating	Comments
1. Eye contact	1 2 3 4 5	
2. Volume of speech	1 2 3 4 5	
3. Rate of speech	1 2 3 4 5	
4. Enthusiasm	1 2 3 4 5	
5. Adherence to time limit	1 2 3 4 5	
6. Absence of vocal fillers	1 2 3 4 5	

Form Grade

Rating Key: 1 – Poor   2 – Fair   3– Good   4= Very Good   5= Excellent

Additional Comments/Suggestions: _____

_____

_____

Persuasive Speech

Purpose: This form is used to evaluate how students can convince their audience to change their opinions/beliefs, feelings and behavior. Students must formulate topics that are interesting and effective.

Name of Student: _____

Date: _____ / _____ / _____

Final Grade

Content	Rating	Comments
1. Choice of topic	1 2 3 4 5	
2. Attention getter	1 2 3 4 5	
3. Statement of purpose	1 2 3 4 5	
4. Body: Supporting evidence	1 2 3 4 5	
5. Conclusion	1 2 3 4 5	
6. Organization/unity of ideas	1 2 3 4 5	
7. Use of visual aids	1 2 3 4 5	

Content Grade

Form	Rating	Comments
1. Posture/Gestures	1 2 3 4 5	
2. Facial expressions	1 2 3 4 5	
3. Tone/Volume of voice	1 2 3 4 5	
4. Enthusiasm	1 2 3 4 5	
5. Time limit	1 2 3 4 5	

Form Grade

Rating Key: 1 = Poor   2 = Fair   3 = Good   4 = Very Good   5 = Excellent

Additional Comments/Suggestions: _____

_____

_____

_____

_____

Debate

Purpose: This form is used to evaluate how students (individual speaker or debating team) can convince the audience to agree with their ideas. Opposite points of view are presented and argued. Therefore, there is a lot of persuading involved. A winner, as an individual or group, must be chosen based on the criteria indicated in the evaluation form.

A. Name of Student/s (Speaker A/Group A): Affirmative:

B. Name of Student/s (Speaker B/Group B): Negative:

Final Grade

Date:_____/_____/_____

Content	Rating A	Rating B	Comments
1. Explanation of proposition	1 2 3 4 5	1 2 3 4 5	
2. Proofs that problem exist	1 2 3 4 5	1 2 3 4 5	
3. Rebuttal	1 2 3 4 5	1 2 3 4 5	
4. Supporting evidence	1 2 3 4 5	1 2 3 4 5	
5. Effectiveness of reasoning	1 2 3 4 5	1 2 3 4 5	
6. Organization/unity of ideas	1 2 3 4 5	1 2 3 4 5	
7. Use of visual aids	1 2 3 4 5	1 2 3 4 5	

Content Grade

Form	Rating	Rating	Comments
1. Posture/Gestures	1 2 3 4 5	1 2 3 4 5	
2. Facial expressions	1 2 3 4 5	1 2 3 4 5	
3. Tone/Volume of voice	1 2 3 4 5	1 2 3 4 5	
4. Enthusiasm	1 2 3 4 5	1 2 3 4 5	
5. Time limit	1 2 3 4 5	1 2 3 4 5	

Form Grade

Rating Key: 1 = Poor   2 = Fair   3= Good   4= Very Good   5= Excellent

Additional Comments/Suggestions: _____

_____

_____

Impromptu Speech

Purpose: This form is used to evaluate how students can convince their audience to change their opinions/beliefs, feelings and behavior. Students must formulate topics that are interesting and effective.

Name of Student: _____

Date: _____ / _____ / _____

Final Grade

Content	Rating					Comments
1. Choice of topic	1	2	3	4	5	
2. Attention getter	1	2	3	4	5	
3. Statement of purpose	1	2	3	4	5	
4. Body: Supporting evidence	1	2	3	4	5	
5. Conclusion	1	2	3	4	5	
6. Organization/unity of ideas	1	2	3	4	5	
7. Use of visual aids	1	2	3	4	5	

Content Grade

Form	Rating					Comments
1. Posture/Gestures	1	2	3	4	5	
2. Facial expressions	1	2	3	4	5	
3. Tone /Volume of voice	1	2	3	4	5	
4. Enthusiasm	1	2	3	4	5	
5. Time limit	1	2	3	4	5	

Form Grade

Rating Key: 1 = Poor   2 = Fair   3= Good   4= Very Good   5= Excellent

Additional Comments/Suggestions: _____

_____

_____

_____

_____

Notes

Notes